The Lost Colony

The Lost Colony
DAN LACY

FRANKLIN WATTS | NEW YORK | LONDON

Maps by Vantage Art, Inc.
Cover design by Appelbaum & Curtis

SBN: 531-00761-8
Copyright © 1972 by Franklin Watts, Inc.
Library of Congress Catalog Card Number: 70-182898
Printed in the United States of America
6 5

Contents

Prologue	*3*
Chapter I	*11*
Chapter II	*23*
Chapter III	*39*
Chapter IV	*64*
Chapter V	*74*
Index	*83*

The Lost Colony

Prologue

John White stared eagerly through the mist that hung over the water. It was a dark night and it was difficult to see the landmarks on the island.

"Halloo!" he shouted. "Halloo!" There was no answer.

He motioned to the trumpeter sitting beside him in the boat, who lifted his horn and blew a familiar naval call. But there was no human sound except the hushed breathing of the men beside him.

He remembered another time when he had come searching to that island and had found only ruined huts and a human skeleton. He tried to conceal the worry in his voice as he told the crew to anchor for the night.

It was a restless night for John White. Tomorrow would be August 18 — August 18, 1590. It would be his granddaughter's third birthday. He remembered the August day in 1587 when his daughter, Eleanor Dare, had presented him with a new granddaughter — the first English child born in the New World.

They had named the little girl Virginia, the same name they gave the new land they came to settle. The name was in honor of Elizabeth, the virgin queen of England.

The baby was less than two weeks old when White had sailed off to England to organize the next year's voyage that would bring more food and more colonists. And then had come the war with Spain and the vast effort of the Spanish fleet — the Invincible Armada — to crush the English navy and to invade England herself. Those were the years when every ship was held at home to defend the island kingdom. This, therefore, would be the first contact with the stranded colonists in three years.

White and his sailors went ashore and pushed through the woods to the inner side of the island looking across the sound to the mainland a few miles away. But the only signs of humans were prints of bare feet in the sand — Indian feet, for Englishmen would have worn some sort of shoes. The tracks looked fresh, as if they had been made during the previous night. Perhaps Indians had been staring at them with silent eyes as they lay anchored off the island and had slipped away before dawn.

John White was more anxious than ever and half ran as he led the men along the beach around the northern point of the island to where the little colony had built its huts. When they reached the site, they scrambled up the bank. At its top was a tree with the letters CRO carved in the bark. CRO and nothing more.

The men quickly pushed through the woods and tangled vines. A strong palisade of trees like a small-scale English fort had been built around the site since White had left three years before. But now all the houses had been taken down. Inside the palisade they found nothing but a few bars of iron and lead and some small cannon and cannonballs — things too heavy for the colonists to carry easily.

On one of the posts of the palisade was carved the word CROATOAN. John White remembered his last words to the colonists. If they moved the colony they were to carve the name of the place to which they were going. And if they were in danger or distress, they were to carve a cross over the name. White looked again and sighed with relief — there was no cross. He knew Croatoan. It was an Indian village on an outer island about fifty miles away that was the home village of a friendly Indian chief, Manteo. Perhaps that was where the colonists were.

White and his men searched the rest of the island for any other clues. Everything else was gone; the small boat (called a "pinnace") that had been left with the colonists, the planks from their houses, some smaller cannon, their clothes, and their household goods.

As White turned to leave the inlet where the colonists had kept the pinnace, some of the sailors came running to say that they had found chests the colonists had left behind. In a ditch were buried five chests, three of which White recognized as his own. The colonists must have tried to conceal them, but the Indians had dug them up and broken them open, scattering the books and pictures and armor to rust and mildew in the rain.

A look at the sky showed dark and threatening clouds. The wind was blowing strong and even in the protected

An etching depicting the scene at Roanoke Island as John White and his men discover that the colonists are missing.
(THE BETTMAN ARCHIVE)

sound the waves were beginning to lash against the shore. It was time to leave. Gathering up a few of the half-ruined paintings and books, White and his men hastened to their boat and rowed for their ships, which were anchored off the inlet in the open ocean. By the time they reached the ships, the storm was so violent that they could scarcely climb aboard the tossing vessels.

White told his tale to the captain of the Hopewell, *the larger of the two ships. They agreed to sail down the coast to Croatoan the next day. But the storm grew worse. The ships had to abandon the casks they had filled with fresh water because the waves were so violent that they could not be brought aboard from the island. Two anchors were lost in the storm and the* Hopewell *was almost driven ashore. The next morning they found that the* Moonlight, *the smaller ship, was leaking badly.*

White and the officers agreed that they could not risk the dangerous shoals around Croatoan. In any event, they did not have enough food left to supply the colonists, even if they did find them. They agreed that the Hopewell *would sail to Trinidad, in the West Indies, to be refitted and to replenish its stock, and then it would return to Croatoan in the spring to find and supply the colony. The injured Moonlight would sail directly for England.*

No doubt John White looked longingly across the raging sea toward Croatoan as they sailed south, for he must have been thinking of his daughter and his granddaughter, and wondering if they were alive.

The Lost Colony

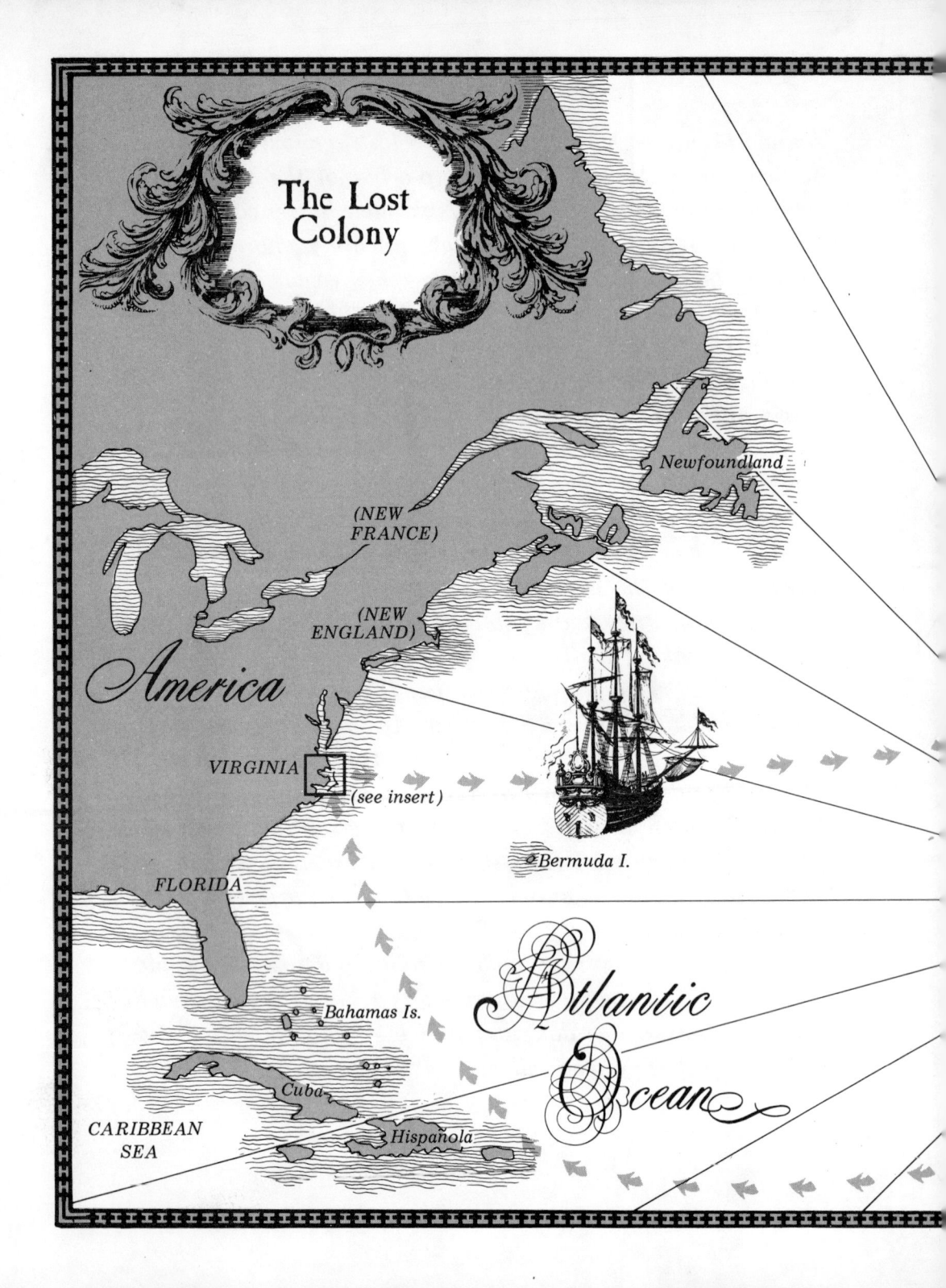

Newfoundland

(NEW FRANCE)

(NEW ENGLAND)

America

VIRGINIA
(see insert)

FLORIDA

Bermuda I.

Bahamas Is.

Cuba

CARIBBEAN SEA

Hispañola

Atlantic Ocean

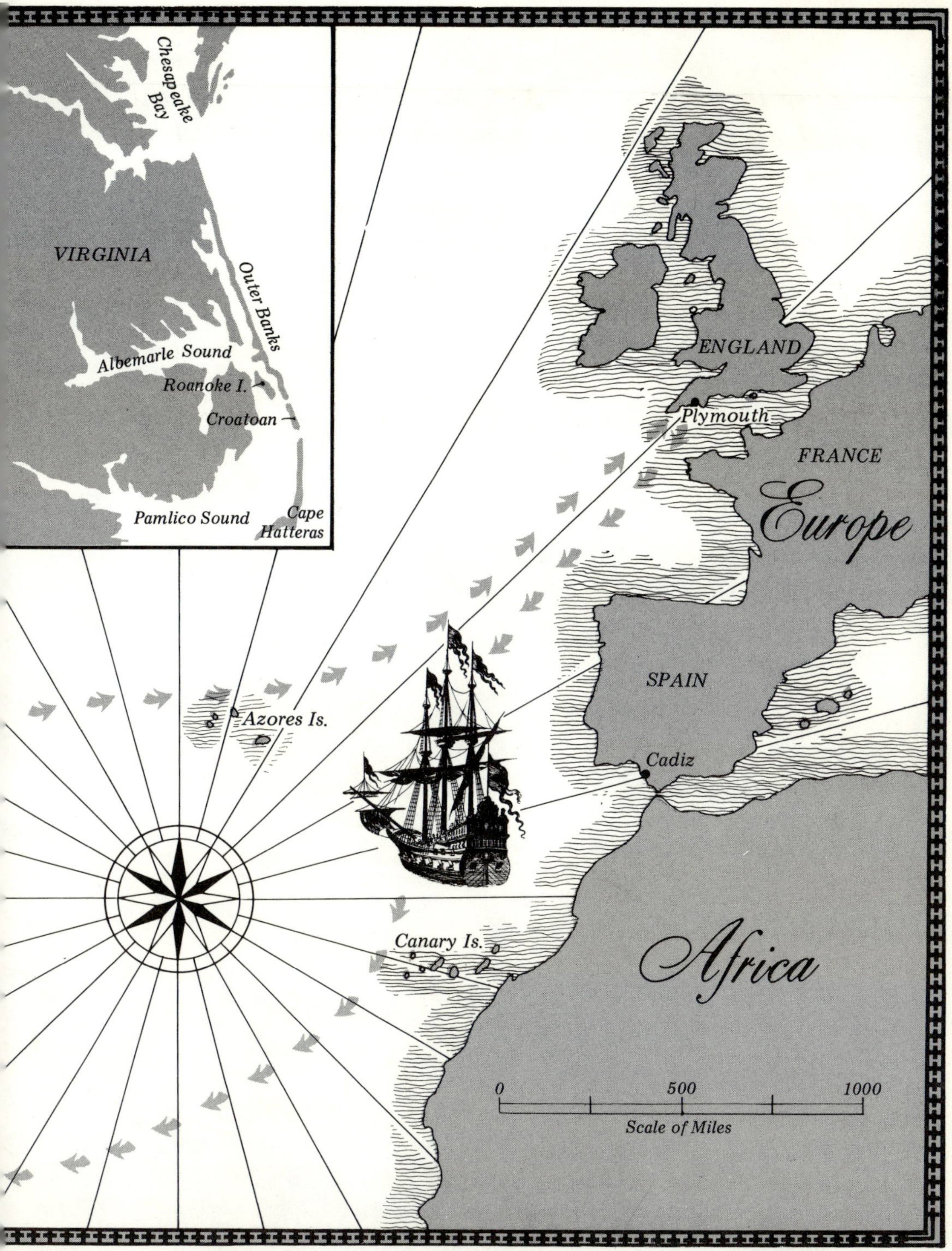
Chesapeake Bay
VIRGINIA
Outer Banks
Albemarle Sound
Roanoke I.
Croatoan
Pamlico Sound
Cape Hatteras
ENGLAND
Plymouth
FRANCE
Europe
SPAIN
Cadiz
Azores Is.
Canary Is.
Africa
0
500
1000
Scale of Miles

Even the plan to go to Trinidad failed. Another violent storm blew the ship far off course and forced her to sail for England by way of the Azores Islands. It was two months later, far into autumn, when they limped into the harbor of Plymouth in southwestern England.

John White never returned to America and never again saw his daughter or his baby granddaughter or all the company of brave men and women he had left on the distant island.

Who were these colonists? What had brought them to the New World? Where had they gone? And what was their mysterious fate?

Chapter I

Spain had first come to the New World shortly after Columbus planted Spain's flag in the Americas in 1492. For nearly a hundred years Spain had been extending her rule over Mexico, Central America, most of South America, and most of the islands of the Caribbean. From this empire their colonists sent back an endless flow of treasures, especially silver, from the mines of Mexico and Peru. These riches had made Spain the world's most powerful empire, paying for fleets of great warships and a strong army.

During these years England had been a weak island nation, torn by civil wars and other internal problems. She had neither the money nor the strength to try to build up an American empire of her own. But by the 1570's this was beginning to change. A slim young queen, Elizabeth I, had come to the throne in 1558, and had won over the hearts of her countrymen as no other ruler of England ever had. She was able to bring to an end the religious and political quarrels that had divided England for so long. With peace came prosperity and confidence and an eagerness for exploration and adventure. It was also the time when Shakespeare and other great poets and playwrights won their fame.

Nothing seemed too difficult to Englishmen then, and they looked with envy at Spain's American empire. Here were the

England
Scotland
Isle of Man
Lancaster
York
North Sea
Lincoln
Derby
Norwich
Severn R.
Nottingham
Cambridge
WALES
Gloucester
Oxford
London
Thames R.
Canterbury
Bristol
DEVON
Exeter
Isle of Wight
CORNWALL
Plymouth
Falmouth
Land's End
English Channel

wonders of strange lands and people, the glory of bold adventure, and treasure such as a poor English boy could scarcely imagine.

The map of England shows a long finger thrusting southwestward into the Atlantic. This peninsula is Cornwall, and the county of Devon borders on the east. The original Britons were driven into this corner of England before the earlier onslaught of Angles and Saxons. They lived in a land of rocky hills and upland moors that were swept by fog. This was where the legendary King Arthur held his court at Camelot and where the oldest traditions of England were rooted. Some of the farmers still spoke the old language, Cornish.

The fields were not as fertile as those in the rest of England, so the hardy west country men looked to the surrounding seas for their living. Many of them had spent their entire lives at sea. Fishing and trading across the stormy North Atlantic, they had developed a new type of ship that was lower, leaner, and faster than the awkward vessels the Spanish used. The galleons of Spain had been patterned on ships built for the calm Mediterranean Sea and for hand-to-hand fighting. The English ships could sail rings around them, and English gunsmiths had made cannon that could outshoot any in the world. With these guns, even light Eng-

Map of England, showing Cornwall peninsula at lower left.

Portrait of Queen Elizabeth in the 1570's by an unknown artist. (NATIONAL PORTRAIT GALLERY, LONDON)

lish ships could keep out of the range of the Spanish galleons and batter them into surrender.

As the English gathered strength under Elizabeth, the bold men of the west country ventured farther and farther into the Atlantic and began to attack and capture Spanish ships. This breed of men became known as "sea dogs," half pirates, half heroes. Some of them, like Sir John Hawkins and Sir Francis Drake, became known and feared across half the world. With increasing boldness they invaded the Spanish islands and ports of the Caribbean, seizing treasure ships and holding towns for ransom. They even raided the Spanish home port of Cadiz, and in Drake's words, "singed the King of Spain's beard."

These raiding voyages were exciting adventures and sometimes they brought great riches. But to snatch bits of treasure from the great wealth of Spain was not enough. Increasingly Englishmen, and especially the bold men of the west, wanted an American empire of their own. And finally one of them came forth who seemed strong enough and determined enough to win it.

This was Sir Walter Raleigh, who was one of the great men of his time. He was a striking man, more than six feet tall when most men were short, and darkly handsome when most men were fair. Even in an age when men of wealth dressed like peacocks, Raleigh outdazzled them all. His armor was silver; gold earrings gleamed through his black curls; jeweled rings glittered on his fingers. None showed to better advantage in the royal court.

IOANNES HAWKINS

Advancement by
diligence

Elizabethan "sea dogs" Sir Francis Drake (below) and Sir John Hawkins (left).

But Raleigh was no idle courtier. As a boy of seventeen he learned the trade of war while fighting in France on behalf of the Huguenots. Though he had had only a brief stay at Oxford University, he had studied law and as an adult had learned all that was known in his day of mathematics, navigation, and geography. He became a learned historian and late in life he wrote an important history of the world. In an age of great poetry, he wrote poetry that was famous in its time and that is remembered and quoted even today.

But somehow Sir Walter Raleigh was more than the sum of all these achievements. He was a proud and arrogant man, and had many enemies. Much later in his life these enemies were to bring about his imprisonment for many years and finally his beheading. But even those who most hated and opposed him spoke of him with awe as the ablest man in England. They seemed to sense a mysterious air about him and there were even those who whispered rumors of witchcraft and ancient magic.

Raleigh's father was a solid west country squire, a moderately wealthy landowner little known outside his own county. But his mother came from a powerful family. Her son by an earlier marriage, Sir Humphrey Gilbert, was Raleigh's much older half-brother. Before Raleigh had ever been presented to Queen Elizabeth, Sir Humphrey was well known in court as an explorer and adventurer to the New

Sir Walter Raleigh. (THE NEW YORK PUBLIC LIBRARY)

Amore et Virtute

ÆTATIS SVÆ 3[?]
AN 1588

World. He had been particularly active in connection with the fisheries off Newfoundland and in explorations in the surrounding area. Through the influence of Sir Humphrey and a cousin who was a lady-in-waiting to the queen, Raleigh came to Elizabeth's attention. He was already known for his military service in France and Ireland, but it was his charm and intelligence that won the queen. When they first met, Elizabeth was past forty-five and Raleigh was not yet thirty, but she immediately made him her favorite. Later, much later, she was to turn against Raleigh when she discovered that he had secretly married one of her maids of honor. But for many years after 1580 she would not let him out of her sight, and he remained important to her until she died. She made him captain of her guard, gave him an estate in Ireland, and assured him of wealth through the grant of monopolies.

Raleigh's special standing at court cut short his own plans for adventure in the New World, for Elizabeth would not allow him to leave her. But it did give him the money to send others where he could not go himself. From the beginning of his role at court to his death in 1618, Raleigh's life was occupied with dreams and plans and expeditions to build an English empire in the New World.

Raleigh's thoughts were first drawn to the New World by his half-brother, Sir Humphrey Gilbert. In 1578 Queen

Sir Humphrey Gilbert, half-brother of Sir Walter Raleigh.

20

HUMFRIDUS GILBERTUS MILES AURATUS

Quid Non

Elizabeth gave Gilbert an exclusive six-year grant to establish colonies north of the Spanish settlements in America. Though he managed to claim the island of Newfoundland for the queen, Gilbert's two expeditions failed and he himself was drowned on the second one in 1584.

On his brother's death, Raleigh, now well established at court, took over the leadership of the effort. Queen Elizabeth issued a new grant to him on much the same terms Gilbert had received, again with a six-year limit.

Chapter II

Raleigh immediately and energetically threw himself into the task of New World exploration. He wanted a more southern colony than his brother's because it would be easier to settle than the icy regions of Newfoundland. An even more important reason for turning to the south was to establish a colony that could also serve as a base for privateers or warships operating against Spain. The small ships of Elizabeth's day could not hold enough supplies for really long voyages. They also required frequent repairing and cleaning. As a result, a ship setting out from England to attack Spanish galleons in the Caribbean could only operate against Spanish ships for a few weeks after the long voyage from its home port before it had to begin the equally long voyage back. If there were an English base in the New World to which privateers or warships could go to obtain supplies and repairs, they could stay in the area indefinitely. But such a base should be away from the coast itself, where it would not be seen by Spanish ships and would therefore be safe from attack.

In 1584 Raleigh sent out an expedition to find such a place. To his regret Elizabeth would not permit him to lead it himself. It was commanded by Captains Philip Amadas and Arthur Barlowe, and John White was one of the com-

A sailing vessel of sixteenth-century England. (THE BETT-MAN ARCHIVE)

pany. There were only two small ships, as they intended only to explore, not to settle. Very little was known of the coast between Maine and Florida, as no voyages had been reported in that area for fifty years. But the expedition had a highly skilled Portuguese pilot, Simon Fernandez, who had often sailed to the New World. They sailed southwest from England and were carried by the trade winds to the Caribbean, and then turned northward.

They first saw the land of North America where the North Carolina coast juts eastward into the Atlantic between Cape Fear and Cape Hatteras. Then as now, a long, almost continuous line of narrow islands lay like a barrier off the North Carolina shores. These islands are known as the Outer Banks. They vary in size from a half-mile to four or five miles wide. They are broken from time to time by inlets through which boats or very small ships can pass into wide, shallow sounds that lie between the islands and the mainland. Occasionally old inlets are closed and new ones are opened by the great storms that sweep up the coast.

Amadas and Barlowe and their two ships crept along these islands for more than one hundred miles. They thought the islands were the mainland and they were looking for a river or an inlet. They finally found an inlet, which was approximately where Oregon Inlet is now. They inched into the channel and anchored their vessels. When they saw the broad sound ahead of them, they realized that what they thought was the mainland was in fact an island chain. As

HONI SOIT QUI MAL Y PENSE

Autore Ioanne With
Sculptore Theodoro
de Bry, Qui et excud.

VIN

Mongoack

SECO
TAN

Cwareuioc
Panauuaioc
Neuustooc
Sectuoc
Secota
Cotan
Aquscogoc
Paquiwp
Pomeiock
Mor
Ta
Mequopen
Tramasquec
Dasamonquepeu

Promontorium tremendum
Wokokon
Croatoan
Hatora
Paquiwoc

Scala leucarum 25
5   10   15   20   25

Americæ pars, Nunc Virginia dicta, primum ab Anglis inuenta, sumtibus Dn. Walteri Raleigh, Equestris ordinis viri Anno Dm̄ M·D·LXXXV regni vero Sereniss: nostræ Reginæ Elisabethæ XXVII Hujus vero Historia peculiari Libro descripta est, additis etiam Indigenarum Iconibus

CHAWANOOK
Ramushonuok
Ohanoock
Metocuuem
Catokinge
Waratan
Mascoming
WEAPEMEOC
Chepanuu
Skicoak
Cheseproor
Cheseprooc sinus
Apasus
Comokee
Pasquenoke
Trinety harbor

OCCIDENS
MERIDIES
SEPTENTRIO
ORIENS

they explored the island, they found the source of the sweet smell that the land breezes had brought out to them while they were still at sea. It was grapes. The great vines, heavy in that season with grapes, covered the islands so that the very waves from the sea washed over them, and they clung to every tree, even the tall cedars that towered above the sand dunes. Amadas and Barlowe solemnly took possession of the land in the names of Queen Elizabeth and Sir Walter Raleigh. As they walked about the island they saw rabbits and deer and all manner of birds. There were cedars and pines and cypress and sassafras and sweet gum trees, all adding to the clean sweet smell that made the islands seem so pleasant.

After they had lain at anchor for two or three days they saw a canoe slowly paddle up the sound. There were three Indians in it. One of them was put ashore and he walked along the beach until he was just opposite the ships. There he stood waiting, silent and bronze, until Captains Amadas and Barlowe, Simon Fernandez, and a few others went ashore in a boat to speak with him. They could make themselves understood only with signs and gestures, but they persuaded the Indian to come aboard the ship with them. He looked about in wonder, drank a glass of wine and tasted

On pages 26 and 27, Theodore de Bry's engraving of John White's map of Virginia. (RARE BOOK DIVISION, THE NEW YORK PUBLIC LIBRARY, ASTOR, LENOX AND TILDEN FOUNDATIONS)

their meat, nodding and smiling with pleasure. Then he went back to his own boat, paddled into the sound, fished a while, and came back with his canoe fully laden with fish, which he divided between the two small English ships.

The next day several larger Indian canoes appeared bearing forty or fifty men. The small band of Englishmen stood waiting nervously, with hands upon their weapons, not knowing whether the Indians came in war or in peace. Again the canoes pulled into shore, but this time the entire party landed. A large mat was taken out and laid along the beach. With great formality one of the Indians sat himself at one end. Four of his followers sat facing him at the other end, and the remainder stood in a circle, where they silently awaited the coming of the Englishmen.

Again the leaders of the English party came ashore, leaving their crews standing by the guns on board ship. But the Indian leader made friendly gestures and motioned to the Englishmen to come and sit beside him. He spoke for a long time in a grave voice. Once in a while one of the four men at the other end of the mat would whisper something softly, but all the rest of his followers kept complete and utter silence while he spoke. His speech was strange, but from his gestures and an occasional word the Englishmen thought they understood most of what he said.

His name, they understood, was Granganimeo and he was the brother of Wingina, king of all the lands about. Wingina had been wounded in a recent battle with other tribes and

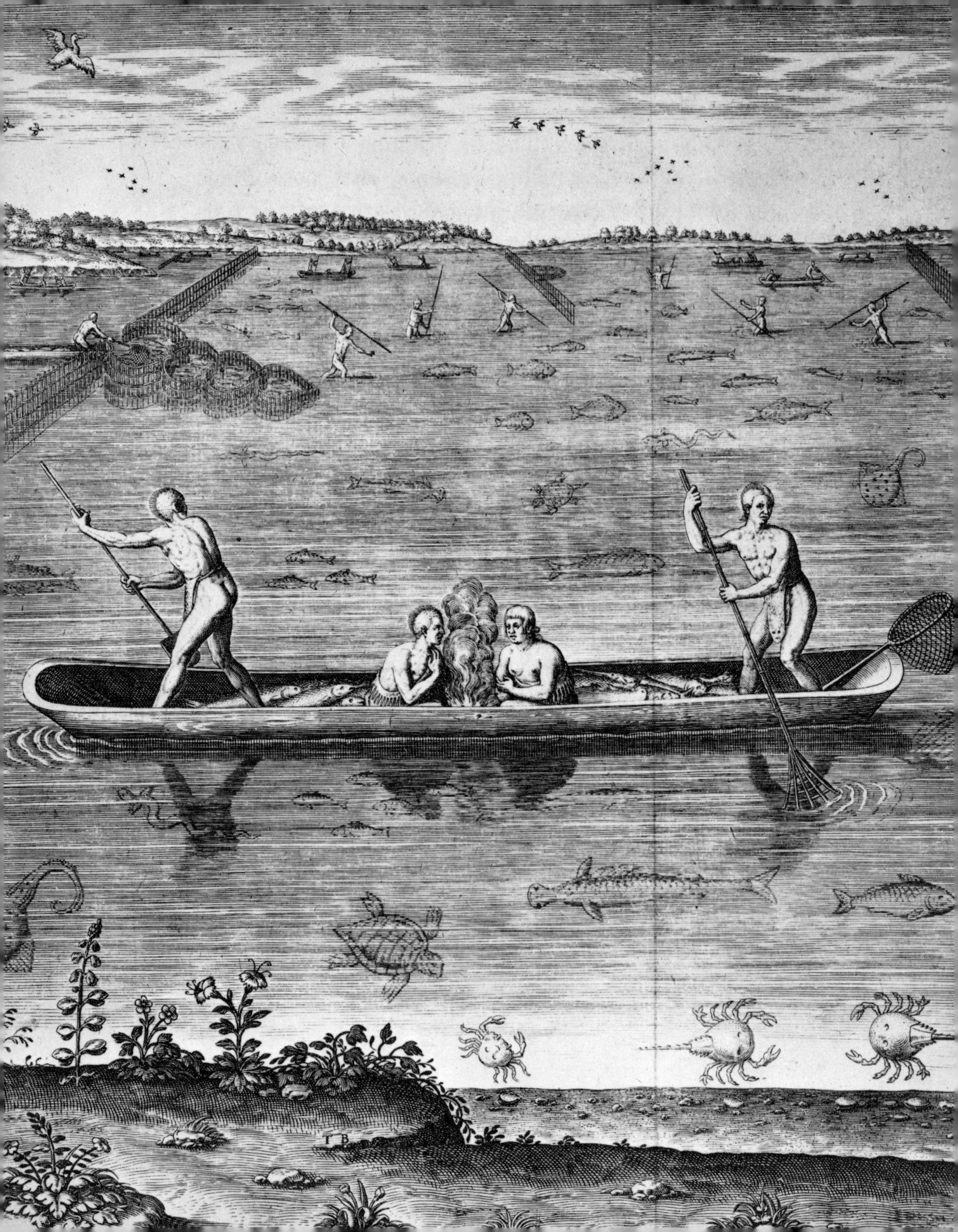

was at his home recovering. The Englishmen were welcome.

They gave the king's brother presents, and then offered others to the four leaders with him. But Granganimeo took all the gifts and put them in his own basket, making stern gestures that the Englishmen were to deal only with him. He rose, the mats were folded, and the Indians walked silently back to their boats. They were impressive men, yellowish-brown rather than red in color, straight and slim, with their heads shaved except for a black strip rising high in the center.

Granganimeo himself had a broad headband of white beads, with a bright plate of copper fastened in the center. (The Englishmen thought at first it might be gold.) He wore a leather loincloth and a leather cloak with the fur inside.

The next day Granganimeo and his band returned. They realized that the English were friendly and had goods to trade. At first they brought deerskins and buffalo hides and traded them for tin plates, which the Indians wanted to use

Theodore de Bry's engraving of John White's painting of the fishing methods of the Indians in North Carolina. Since the Indians did not have iron or steel, they made spears by fastening the sharp tail of a crablike fish to the end of a reed or long rod. They also made fish traps of reeds or sticks as shown in the background of the engraving. (RARE BOOK DIVISION, THE NEW YORK PUBLIC LIBRARY, ASTOR, LENOX AND TILDEN FOUNDATIONS)

as shields, and brass kettles. Later they saw that the English were interested in more than furs, and they brought shells and dyes and pearls, which they traded for metal tools — hatchets, axes, and knives.

The Indians dearly wanted swords, for they had only soft copper from which they could not make weapons or tools, but the English would not trade away their swords. The Indians understood the use of swords because a Spanish ship had wrecked along the coast twenty years before, and from it they had rescued some knives and hatchets and made others from pieces of iron saved from the wreck. But those were used up or lost, and they had had to return to painful work with nothing but shells as tools and with simple weapons of wood, bone, or stone.

After a few more days had passed, Captain Barlowe and seven of his men took the ship's boat to explore the sound. They came to an island that the Indians called Roanoke, which was inside the sound, behind the Outer Banks. On the island was Granganimeo's village, and his wife welcomed them warmly. She and her servants fed them and dried their wet clothes, and urged them to stay the night in the village. The Englishmen still feared the Indians, however, and slept cramped and uneasy in their boat.

The visit to the island gave them a chance to see how the Indians lived. It seemed like a paradise to the English. The earth gave food abundantly, the climate was warm and gentle, and the Indians seemed loving and free from care.

They sampled the various Indian foods and knew that they had venison (the meat of deer) and fish and corn and various kinds of fruits and melons. They planted peas and saw them begin to sprout quickly and thus knew that English plants could grow there.

With signs and gestures the Indians told them of the mainland twenty miles or more away, of the great rivers that ran down into the sound, and of the various villages and chiefs. And all the while the talk went on, the Indian men and women shyly touched the white skin of the Englishmen and their strange clothes, then whispered among themselves. Were they gods? Or ghosts returned to Earth? Or powerful men of great magic? Whatever they were, they were mighty and wonder-working, and it was important to please them and not make them angry. And please them they did. When Captain Barlowe returned to England, he wrote:

> We were entertained with all love, and kindness, and with as much bounty, after their manner, as they could possibly devise. We found the people most gentle, loving, and faithful, void of all guile, and treason, and such as lived after the golden age. The earth bringeth forth all things in abundance, as in the first creation, without toil or labor. The people only care to defend themselves from the cold, and in their short winter, and to feed themselves with such meat as the soil affordeth.

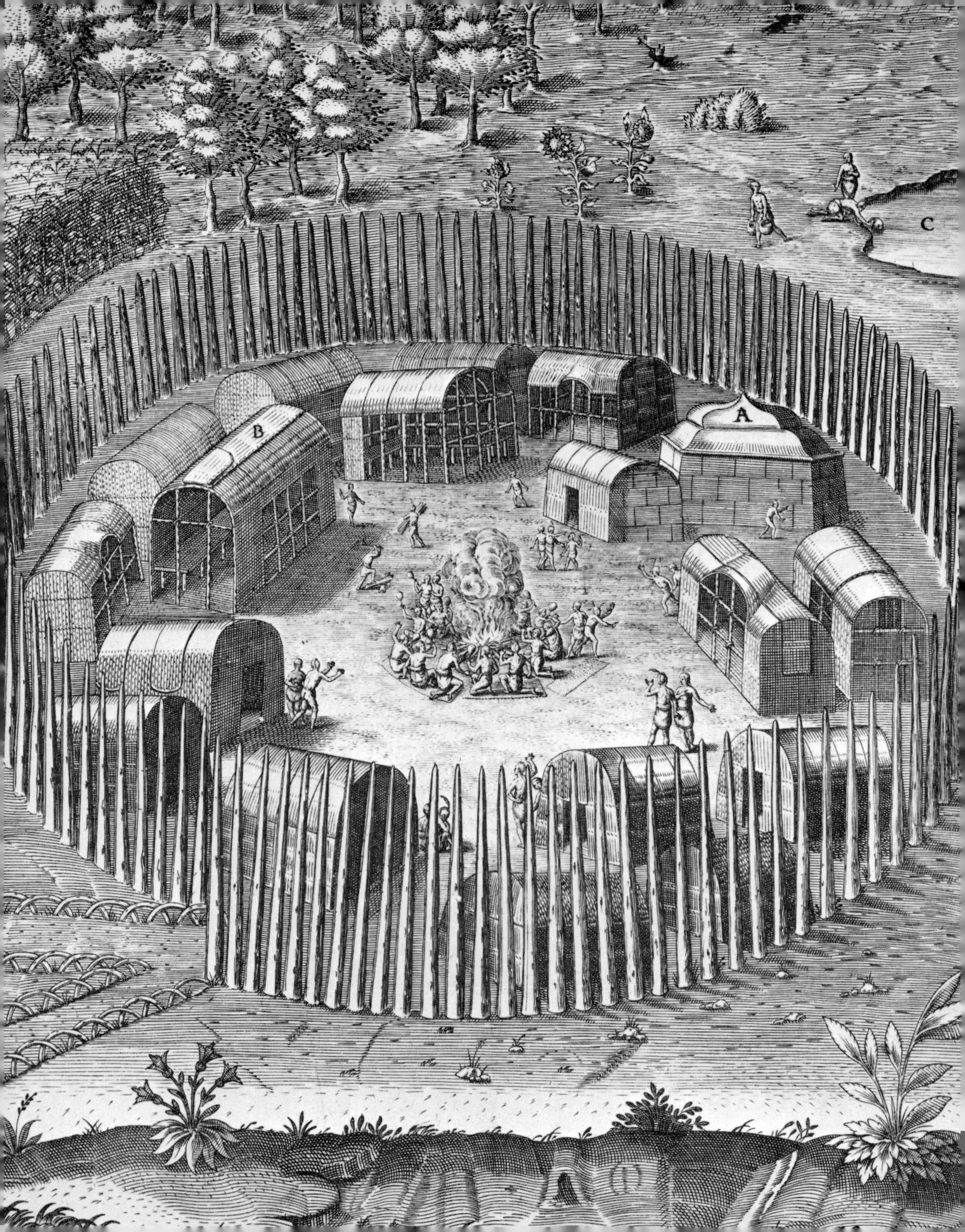

A
B
C

After a few more days Amadas and Barlowe and their men set sail for England to report to Raleigh on the delights and wonders they had found. Their discovery fulfilled Raleigh's hopes completely. The Indians were friendly, the land healthy and fertile, and food abundant — or so the report said.

In addition to being a good site for a colony, it was something more. The Spanish treasure fleets had to lumber up the coast, following the Gulf Stream until they reached a point where the winds blew steadily from west to east and would carry them across the Atlantic. They would pass not far off the coast Amadas and Barlowe had explored. One advantage of this site would be that fast privateers sailing out from the inlets behind the Outer Banks could easily capture them. Another advantage would be that an English base on Roanoke Island would be hidden from Spanish eyes and could be kept a secret. Even if the Spaniards learned its loca-

De Bry's engraving of the Indian town of Pomeiock, located near what is today Engelhard, North Carolina. The building marked "A" at the right side of the village was the temple. The king lived in the building marked "B." The dwellings were made of posts covered with mats or branches of trees. The area marked "C" at the upper right was the pool which the Indians dug to supply the village with fresh water. (RARE BOOK DIVISION, THE NEW YORK PUBLIC LIBRARY, ASTOR, LENOX AND TILDEN FOUNDATIONS)

tion, the base would be protected against surprise attack because the Spanish ships would have to make their way slowly through the inlet before they could reach the sound, and the larger ships would not be able to get through at all.

Two men who returned to England with Amadas and Barlowe were Indians — Manteo and Wanchese. How brave they must have been! They made a far more daring voyage, to a world far stranger to them, than the voyage Raleigh's men had made to Roanoke. All England was excited by them. They quickly learned a little English, and Raleigh used them to speak to groups to build up interest in his colony.

Theodore de Bry's engraving of the town of Secota, located on the bank of the Pamlico River, in what is today Beaufort County, North Carolina. The village scene shows some of the agricultural achievements of the Indians. The area marked "F" in the upper right corner is a man stationed in a hut to frighten the birds and animals away from the corn and tobacco crops ("E"). Other plantings include pumpkins ("I") and flowers ("N"). The large building at the lower left marked "A" was the burial place for the chieftains. The circular area marked "B" was where the Indians prayed, while "C" was the central gathering place in the village. (RARE BOOK DIVISION, THE NEW YORK PUBLIC LIBRARY, ASTOR, LENOX AND TILDEN FOUNDATIONS)

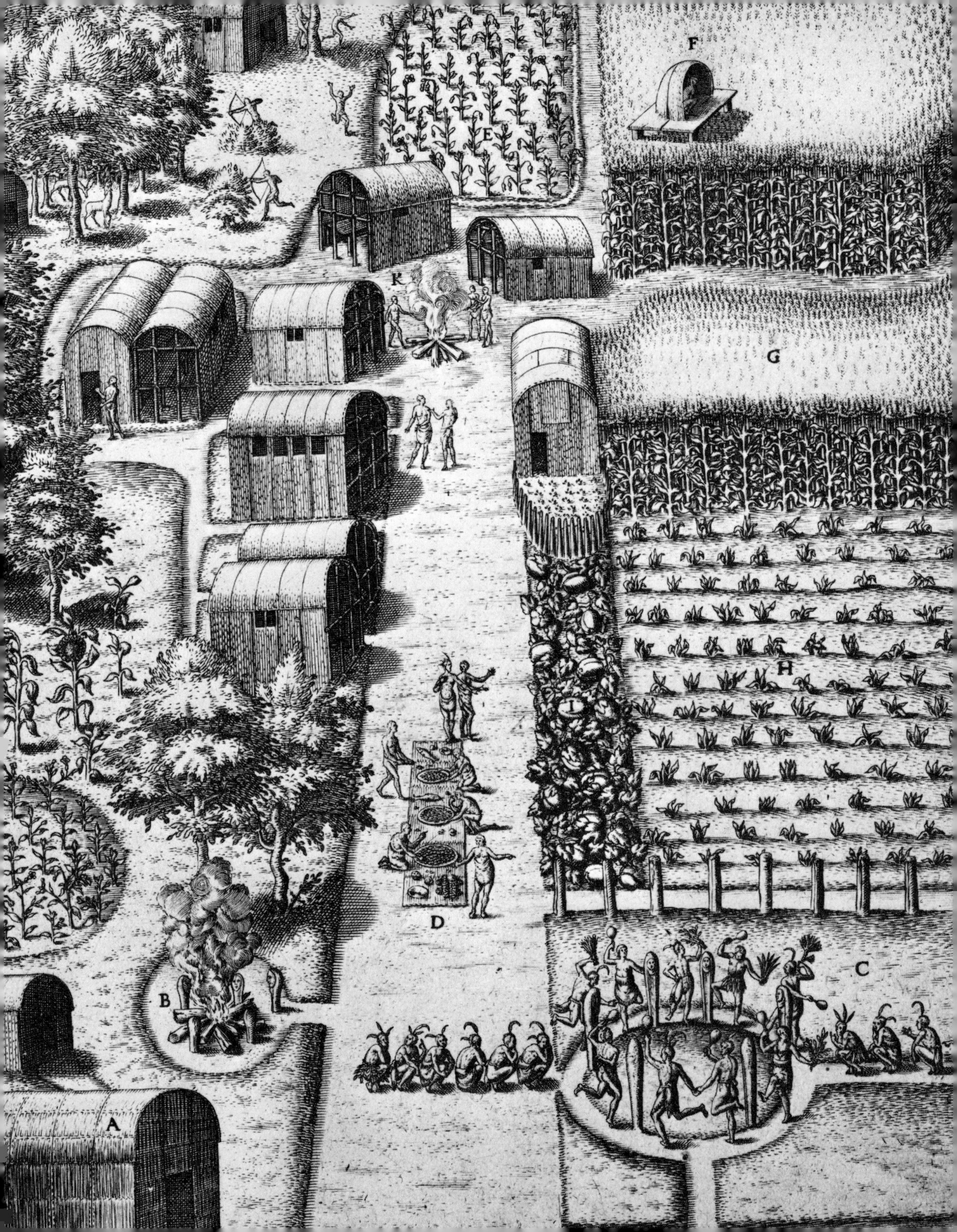
F
E
K
G
H
I
D
C
B
A

He was now determined to plant a permanent settlement in the New World. Even before Amadas and Barlowe had returned with their enthusiastic report, he had begun preparations for a new voyage. He had asked for a law confirming his grant from Queen Elizabeth. He had encouraged his friend Richard Hakluyt, who was the greatest propagandist for the New World, to produce a pamphlet supporting a settlement. And Raleigh arranged to have one of the most brilliant young scientists in England, Thomas Hariot, come live with him and teach him mathematics and navigation.

Chapter III

The pearls, furs, Indians, and enthusiasm brought back by Amadas and Barlowe helped win support for a really major expedition in 1585. Six hundred men in seven ships were assembled. They were put under the command of Sir Richard Grenville, because Queen Elizabeth still would not let Raleigh go himself. Simon Fernandez was the chief pilot again, and several men who were on the 1584 voyage of exploration sailed once more. Among them were Philip Amadas and John White, Thomas Hariot, the scientist, who went to report on the land and the Indians, and Manteo and Wanchese.

The expedition sailed from Plymouth in April. Raleigh had planned to send a second expedition in June, with more supplies and settlers, but trouble arose with Spain, and the ships had to be sent to Newfoundland and put to other uses.

As was normal in those days, the little fleet sailed with the trade winds to the Caribbean, planning to follow the Gulf Stream up the coast. But the ships of the fleet had been separated in a storm, so when they stopped in Puerto Rico to get fresh food and water and to repair their ships, Grenville had with him only his flagship, the *Tiger*, another vessel, the *Elizabeth*, and a Spanish ship he had captured en route.

By trading with the half-hostile Spaniards in Puerto Rico,

Mil. aur.

RICHARDVS GRENVILVS

the men bought cattle, hogs, horses, and additional supplies for the new colony. They also collected breadfruit and other tropical trees and shrubs to replant at the new colony.

The little band then sailed north for Roanoke where they found a new inlet, called Wococon, which was below the present-day Ocracoke. Some of the other ships were already there, so most of the expedition was reunited.

The inlet was very shallow and all the ships had trouble getting through it. The biggest ship, the *Tiger*, ran completely aground and was nearly battered to pieces by the waves. It was finally worked loose from the sandbar, but not before salt water had broken through and damaged most of the supplies they had planned to leave for the new colony. This was a serious blow. Nevertheless, Amadas was sent exploring with the pinnace and discovered rivers flowing into the sound that were not known before, as well as large Indian villages on the mainland.

During these first days of Grenville's expedition, while the advance party under Amadas was still exploring the sound, came the first break in the peaceful relations with the Indians. A silver cup was found to be missing after a party of Indians had visited an English ship. Grenville was a fierce man, determined to show the Indians from the first that they could not dare oppose the white man. He sent Amadas

Sir Richard Grenville.

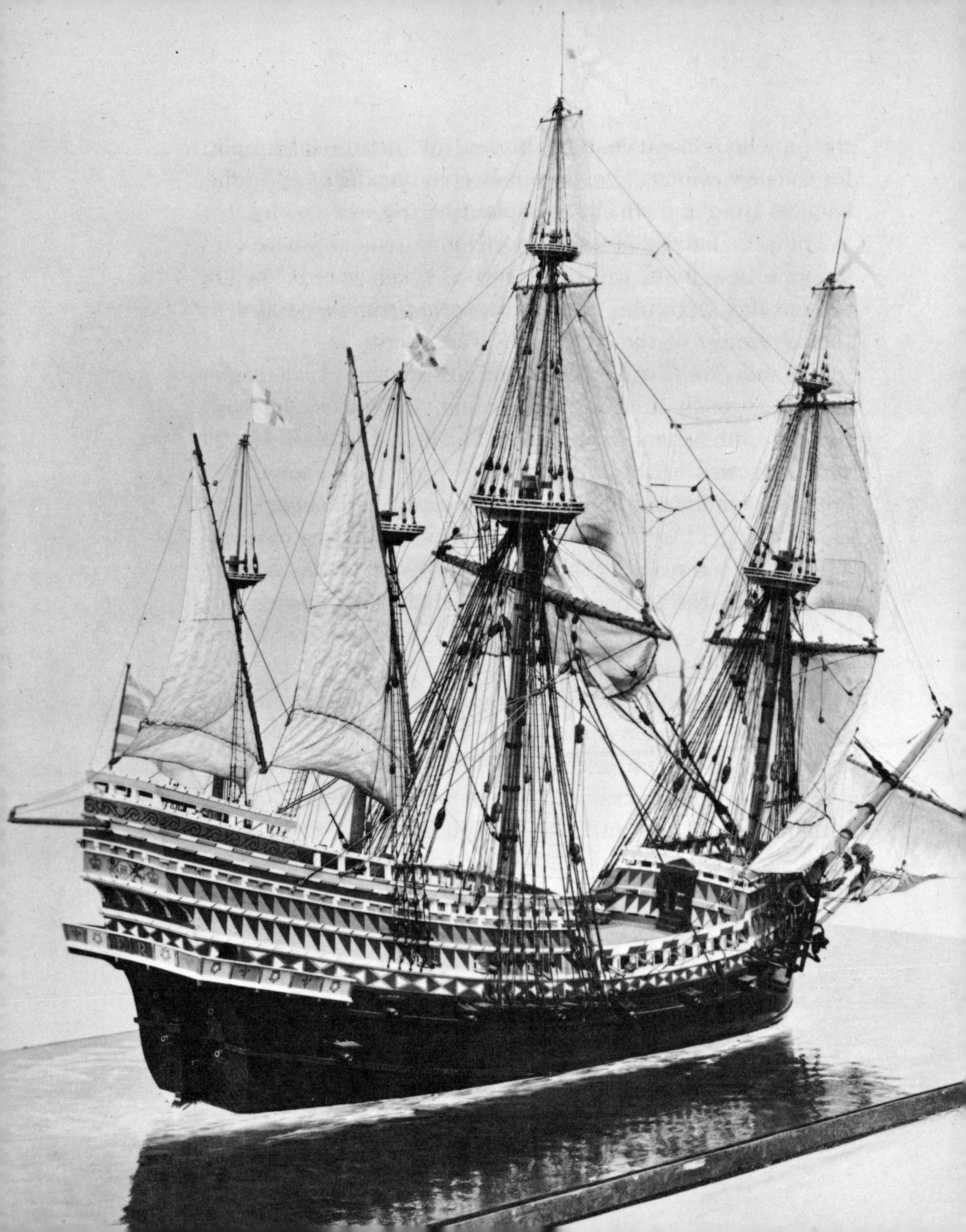

back to the village where that band of Indians lived, with orders to recover the cup and punish those who were guilty. Amadas found that the village was deserted and the cup was not to be found. In revenge Grenville burned the village to the ground and then to further punish the Indians he destroyed all the crops in the field on which they would depend for food during the winter.

This was the first time the Indians of the area had seen the whites act in a cruel and hostile manner. Grenville had meant to fill them with fear. He accomplished this, but he also filled them with hatred.

At first it was far easier on this voyage to deal with and learn from the Indians than it had been on the previous voyage. Manteo and Wanchese now spoke some English, and Thomas Hariot had probably learned from them some of the Indian tongue. With Manteo's help they spoke to their old friend Granganimeo and to his brother, King Wingina. The English gained permission to settle their colony on Roanoke Island, right next to Wingina's village. No one knows why Wingina consented. Perhaps he did not realize how much the English would depend on his people for food. Perhaps he gained a promise of their help against his ene-

The British Science Museum's miniature reproduction of a sixteenth-century British sailing vessel. (BRITISH CROWN COPYRIGHT. SCIENCE MUSEUM, LONDON)

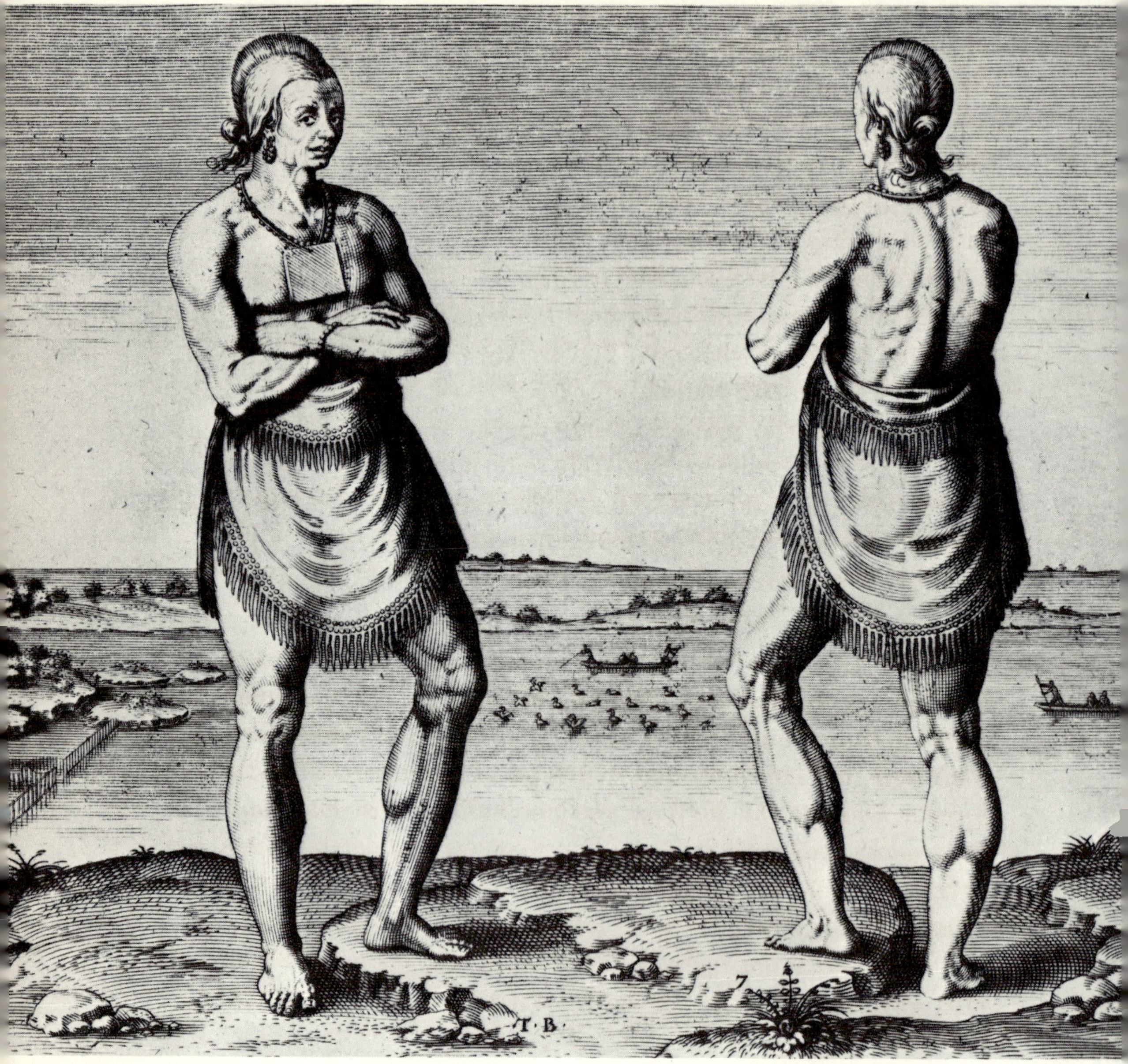
7
T.B.

mies on the mainland. Perhaps, in the face of the guns and cannon of the strange and magic men, he felt he had no choice.

In the course of exploration, it soon became clear that the shallow inlets, which had been ample for the little vessels Amadas and Barlowe had brought the year before, could not provide a harbor in which Grenville could winter with his ships. However suitable for a colony, Roanoke would never provide the base for privateers for which Raleigh had hoped.

Hence Grenville decided to return to England with the ships and to leave only one hundred men under Ralph Lane to build the colony over the winter. The Indians had spoken of a rich land on a great sea to the north, which they called Chesapeake. The colonists would keep a pinnace with which they could explore inland waters. Over the winter they would look for Chesapeake. The next spring or summer Grenville

De Bry's engraving from John White's watercolor of a Roanoke chieftain — perhaps even Wingina. The chieftains wore their hair in a coxcomb on top but let the rest grow long to form a knot at the back of the neck. They did not paint themselves, but wore a chain of pearls or a copper pendant as a sign of authority. The pose of one arm crossed over the other was considered a sign of wisdom. The chieftain's clothing was made from fringed deerskin. (RARE BOOK DIVISION, THE NEW YORK PUBLIC LIBRARY, ASTOR, LENOX AND TILDEN FOUNDATIONS)

promised to return with more settlers and supplies. They could then decide whether the permanent colony would be Roanoke or Chesapeake.

The ships had been moved to the inlet (now Oregon Inlet) near Roanoke where Amadas and Barlowe had anchored the year before. Some weeks were spent unloading supplies and building a small star-shaped earth fort on Roanoke. As the unloading was finished, Grenville's ships left a few at a time. The last one sailed in September, leaving Lane and his men to face the winter in the strange land.

They had a far harder time than Amadas and Barlowe had had in that golden summer of 1584. The main party was able to maintain itself over the winter of 1585–86 in the fort and huts adjoining Wingina's village, living off its own limited supplies and then demanding more and more food from Indian neighbors. Meanwhile, a number of the colonists, probably using the pinnace, had been sent to explore the

De Bry's engraving from White's painting of an annual great feast. The Indians from the entire area came dressed in strange costumes and danced around poles carved with faces. Three of the most beautiful women of the area danced around in the center of the circle while the men and women of the various towns would sing and dance around the perimeter. (RARE BOOK DIVISION, THE NEW YORK PUBLIC LIBRARY, ASTOR, LENOX AND TILDEN FOUNDATIONS)

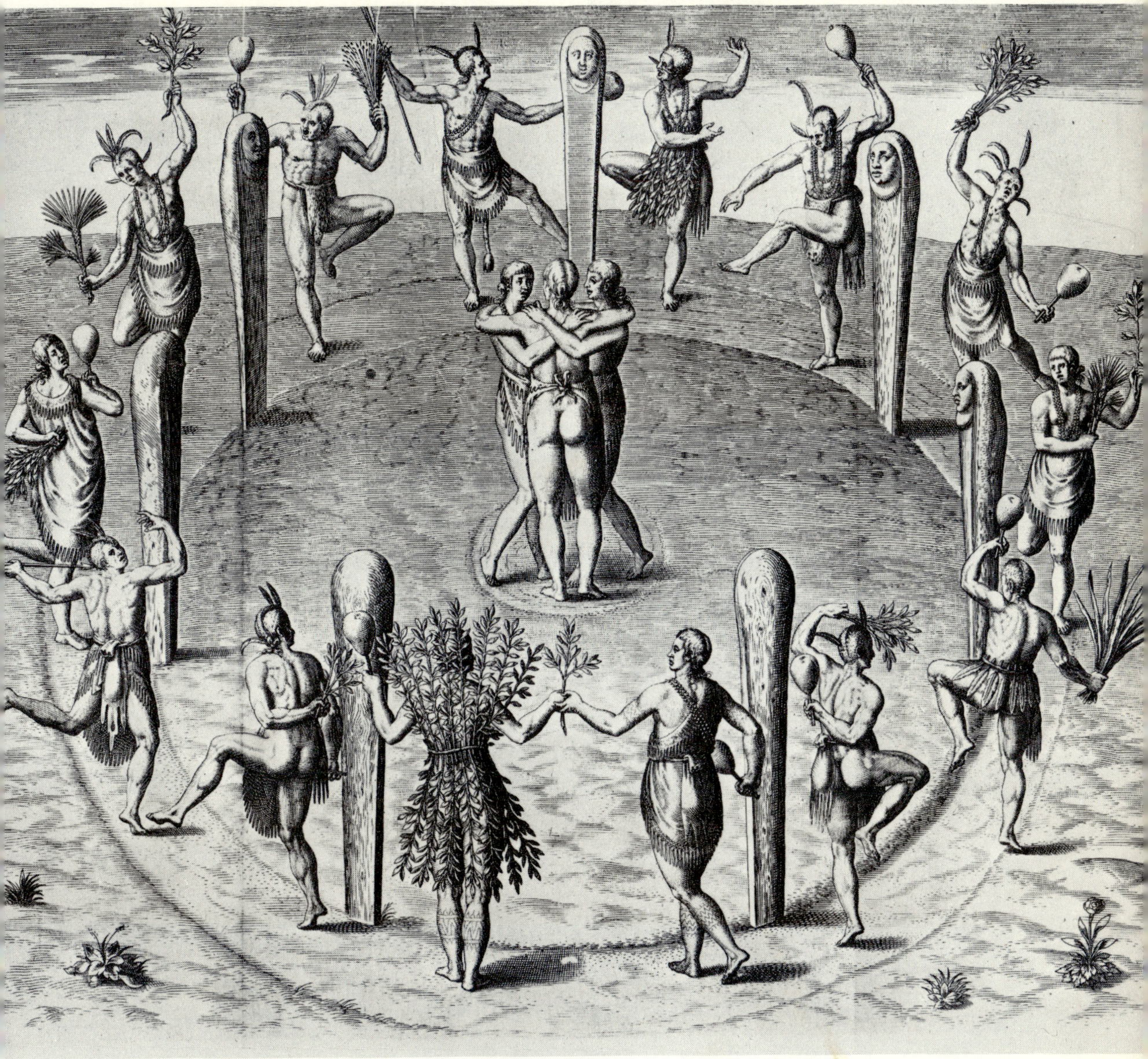

waters to the north. They were seeking the rich land of Chesapeake. They skirted the south edge of Chesapeake Bay and discovered Lynnhaven Bay, between what are now Norfolk and Virginia Beach. It was a far more promising site for a colony, with an excellent deep-water harbor.

By the time this group returned from Chesapeake, the settlers on Roanoke Island were in desperate need of supplies. Their own food was nearly gone, and the Indians' supplies were probably very low. It would be summer before new crops could be harvested.

Wingina, meanwhile, had become more and more hostile. He and his tribesmen resented the constant demands for food they could not spare, and Lane's harsh policies only served to frighten them further. Wingina came to realize that this time the white men were not visitors who would soon leave, but settlers who meant to stay forever and who expected other white men to come and join them. He began to fear for his homeland and to plot as best he could to save it. He visited or sent messengers to all the tribes around, even those who had been his enemies.

After the Chesapeake explorers had rejoined the main group, Lane himself set out with a group of men to explore the Roanoke and Chowan rivers to the northwest. He hoped to bring back stores of food and to learn more about the country. Wingina encouraged him to make the expedition. But he also tried to call together many Indians of different tribes to meet near the mouth of the Chowan. He had sent messages to them that Lane and the Englishmen meant to destroy them, thus hoping to force a fight in which the white men would be destroyed.

But Lane, who had learned of this plan, burst bodily on the gathering before it had completed its plans, and seized Menatonon, the crippled local chief. He also took the chief's son hostage and sent him back to Roanoke by boat. Then Lane continued his explorations up the Chowan and Roanoke rivers. Menatonon had told him there was a bright metal (Lane assumed it was gold) up the Chowan.

Wingina's plan had failed, but he had another. He feared the guns and swords of the English, but he knew they were, in Indian eyes, nearly as helpless as babies in getting food for themselves. He would try to starve them to death. His messengers went silently up the river ahead of Lane's men, warning the tribes in every village to go back into the forest, taking with them all their food and supplies.

And so, as Lane's two boats paddled mile after weary mile up the broad Roanoke, they found nothing but ghost villages. The huts stood empty of men, women, and children. They searched the silent paths and burst into the open huts, but there was nothing — no meat, no corn, no beans, no pumpkins. There was only the dark forest and the knowledge that behind every tree there might be an Indian waiting, arrow on bowstring.

T·B

3

The Englishmen were brave, and they pushed boldly on until their food was nearly gone. But finally they had to row weakly back downstream, half starving. They were even forced to kill and eat a pet dog.

When Lane's weary group staggered back to Roanoke alive, Wingina thought it must have been magic that preserved them. For a while he concealed his purpose, and agreed to show them how to plant corn. But that was March, and it would be many weeks before the ripened crop could ease their hunger. In the meantime they were still dependent on the Indians.

Wingina seized on this dependence. He simply moved with his tribesmen from the village on Roanoke to another village he ruled on the mainland. This was called Dasemonkepeuk, and was about where Mann's Harbor is now. Once out of reach of the English guns, he stopped supplying food. To feed his men, Lane had to divide them, sending some to Croatoan near Cape Hatteras, where there was then an inlet, and others to Oregon Inlet, where the ships had been anchored. Both parties could live from fishing and collecting oysters and clams, and perhaps from food given by the

De Bry's engraving of a chieftain with his bow and arrow and quiver of rushes. The Indians used the bow and arrow for hunting and battle. (RARE BOOK DIVISION, THE NEW YORK PUBLIC LIBRARY, ASTOR, LENOX AND TILDEN FOUNDATIONS)

friendly Indians of Croatoan, Manteo's home village. Lane sent still others to the mainland where they could dredge up oysters and eat cassava, a starchy food made from the roots of a plant that grew wild there.

In this way Lane kept his men from starving. But he had to divide his forces, which was what Wingina expected. The chief went to the other tribes to win their support. They agreed to gather on July 10, when some of Wingina's bravest followers would slip over to Roanoke Island during the night and kill Lane. With their leader dead, the other Englishmen, divided into small groups, could easily be captured or killed.

It was a skillfully made plan, but it was betrayed to Lane by some Indians who were either genuinely friendly to him or who were afraid of him. With this news, Lane decided to attack the Indians before they could attack him. His first thought was to entice Wingina to Roanoke Island, where he could seize him. But the Indian leader was too clever to walk into a trap like that. Lane's next plan was to announce that

A de Bry engraving showing the symbols worn by the Indians to identify whose subjects they were and what town they were from. The four-arrow symbol marked "A" was that of Wingina, the chief of Roanoke. (RARE BOOK DIVISION, THE NEW YORK PUBLIC LIBRARY, ASTOR, LENOX AND TILDEN FOUNDATIONS)

23.

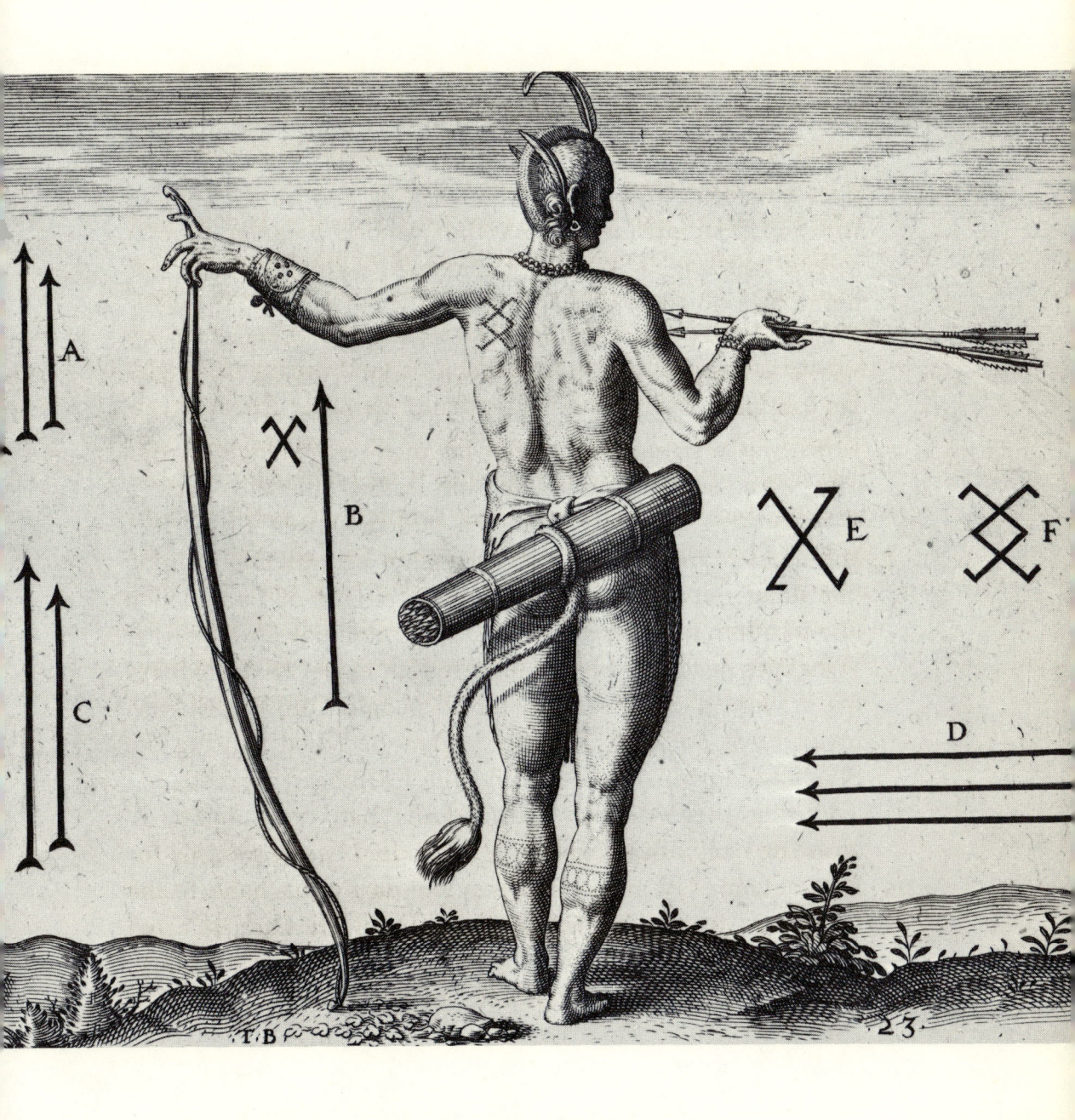

his party was leaving Roanoke for Croatoan, but instead to slip over to the mainland by night and attack Wingina's men while they slept. This, too, failed, because some of Lane's men were seen from the shore attacking and killing Indians who were attempting to leave the island in a canoe in order to give warning. The Indians remained watchful during the night, and no surprise was possible.

On the next day Lane and some of his bravest men went boldly to Wingina's village and demanded to see the king. While they were talking, Lane cried, "Christ our victory!" which was a signal, and one of his men shot Wingina while others fired into his Indian followers, killing them all. Though shot through the body, Wingina pulled himself to his feet and fled toward the forest. He was shot again while running but staggered into the sheltering trees. One of Lane's men followed him into the dark forest and came out later bearing Wingina's head. He was the first Indian leader that died trying in vain to save his land and his people from the English invaders, as hundreds of other leaders had died fighting the Spaniards in Mexico, Peru, and the Caribbean Islands.

During these difficult weeks Lane had been anxiously awaiting Grenville's relief fleet, which had been promised for Easter. One of his reasons for sending part of his band to the inlets was to watch for the hoped-for fleet. Lane realized that Roanoke, reached only by shallow and dangerous inlets, and now surrounded by hostile tribes, was an impossible place for the colony and privateering base that Raleigh wanted. As soon as Grenville came with reinforcements, it was Lane's plan to build a fort and colony in the Chesapeake area and move the settlement there. The Indians had told Lane that he could also reach Chesapeake by going up the Chowan River and then making a short journey overland. He proposed to find and open a trail that would provide such an overland link from the proposed new colony to the Chowan River so that the colonists could explore for the copper and gold they had been told could be found at the river's source.

Within a few days after the final fight with Wingina, the welcome news came. Lane's lookouts at the inlet had sighted a large fleet that they assumed must be Grenville's. To their surprise, however, the ships turned out to be not Grenville's, but Sir Francis Drake's. Drake commanded a fleet that had sailed from England in the fall of 1585 to attack the Spanish in the Caribbean. He had looted Santo Domingo and Cartagena and threatened to seize Havana and the Isthmus of Panama. Finishing his expedition, he had started home for England sailing north in the Gulf Stream. After seizing St. Augustine, in what is now Florida, he reached what is today the North Carolina coast and made contact with Lane's men at Croatoan on June 8.

Drake anchored in Oregon Inlet and offered the colonists what he could. He was well equipped, for he had brought

55

enough supplies to establish a base on the Isthmus of Panama, which he had not accomplished, and he had also seized a good deal of material at St. Augustine.

Drake offered to leave a small ship, some boats, mariners, and equipment, and enough food to carry Lane's men through the summer and into autumn. With these resources, Lane could move the colony to Chesapeake and sail to England himself to seek further aid.

All was agreed and the supplies were being moved ashore and onto the *Francis*, the ship Drake had offered, when one of the sudden storms of the southern coast hurled itself upon the little fleet. Drake's ships were scattered, many of the supplies were lost, and the *Francis* disappeared into the storm.

This took away whatever heart was left in Lane and his men. They decided to abandon the colony and sail home with Drake, who had been able to round up all of his ships except the *Francis*. On June 18 or 19 they sailed. Three Englishmen who had been hunting in the interior were left behind and nobody knows their fate. Manteo decided to return to England and sailed with Lane's men.

Their ships had hardly disappeared over the horizon when Raleigh's advance ship, sent ahead of Grenville's fleet, dropped anchor in Oregon Inlet. If Lane had waited even one or two more days, he would have gained the support that would have enabled him to hold out. Grenville's entire fleet was there by mid-July. If Lane had stayed and moved the settlement as he had planned, Lane's colony and not Jamestown would probably be remembered as the first permanent English settlement in the New World.

Finding the colony gone, Grenville's smaller ships explored the sound and rivers but of course found no trace of Lane's men. At first, Grenville found no Indians either, as they had learned that their best defense against the white man was to disappear. When he was finally able to come upon an Indian who was willing to talk, he learned that the colonists had left in English ships. He guessed correctly that it was Drake's fleet.

Grenville had enough men to reestablish the colony in force, but he decided instead to leave only fifteen men to hold the fort for another year. He left with them abundant supplies and four light cannon in the still-standing earth fort Lane's men had built. Because all English expeditions to the New World were as much for privateering as for colonizing, Grenville set sail as soon as possible in the hopes of capturing some Spanish treasure ships on his way home to England.

Lane's colony half failed, half succeeded. They brought back disappointing news of the dangers of the inlets and harbors near Roanoke, and what they had to tell of the hostile Indians was very different from the tales of the gentle and friendly natives brought back by Amadas and Barlowe.

T. P.   17.

Lane's aggressive behavior and demands for food the Indians could ill spare had done much to make enemies of them. But it had been proved that Englishmen could survive a year in the wilderness, and that the land was healthy and fertile. Pearls and furs had been found, and there existed the possibility of finding copper or gold. There was also the news of much more promising sites in the Chesapeake area.

And they brought back with them another kind of priceless treasure: John White's drawings and Thomas Hariot's scientific notes. The artist and the scientist made a good team. While others fought or hunted or tried their hands at planting, White and Hariot had gone about looking, noting, and asking questions of the Indians. White was a gifted artist and he sketched all he saw: the plants, the birds, the fish, the animals, and especially the Indians. He drew a chief, probably Wingina himself, tall and proud, with the stiff strip of hair rising from his head that was shaved high on the sides, with earrings and bracelets and a necklace of pearls and the

This de Bry engraving shows how the Indians built their boats They first made a fire at the base of a tree which eventually caused the tree to fall. Then they stripped off the bark and upper branches and placed the trunk on a platform. After burning out the center of the trunk, they scraped the charred wood away with shells. (RARE BOOK DIVISION, THE NEW YORK PUBLIC LIBRARY, ASTOR, LENOX AND TILDEN FOUNDATIONS)

AN DNI 1602
TATIS SVÆ 32

great plate of shining copper hanging on his chest. He drew princesses and ordinary Indians, too, with their deerskin robes and tattooed skin. He pictured them fishing and planting crops and dancing, and drew the strange costume of their medicine men. These drawings were as great a wonder to the men of that day as the photographs brought back from the moon were to us.

White's original drawings have been lost. Perhaps he discarded them as preliminary sketches after he had made finished copies on his return to England. One set of those copies, made by White himself, is now in the British Museum in London. Another set was reproduced in engravings made by Theodore de Bry for a book published in 1590. Even before de Bry's book allowed the public to see the drawings, they were surely passed from hand to hand among the queen's advisers and the men of wealth who might invest in a new colony.

Thomas Hariot on his return wrote "A Briefe and True Report of the New Found Land of Virginia." It was a thorough, scientific, and accurate account of what he had actually seen, but it was so written as to encourage people to invest and settle in the new colony. He described in words much

This portrait by an unknown artist hangs at Trinity College, Oxford, and is believed to be that of Thomas Hariot. (THE PRESIDENT AND FELLOWS OF TRINITY COLLEGE, OXFORD)

ADMIRANDA NARRATIO
FIDA TAMEN, DE COMMODIS ET
INCOLARVM RITIBVS VIRGINIAE, NVPER
ADMODVM AB ANGLIS, QVI À DN. RICHARDO
GREINVILE EQVESTRIS ORDINIS VIRO EO IN
COLONIAM ANNO. M.D.LXXXV. DEDVCTI SVNT
INVENTAE, SVMTVS FACIENTE DN. VVALTERO
RALEIGH EQVESTRIS ORDINIS VIRO FODINARV
STANNI PRAEFECTO EX AVCTORITATE
SERENISSIMAE REGINAE ANGLIAE.

ANGLICO SCRIPTA SERMONE
A THOMA HARIOT, EIVSDEM WALTERI DOMESTI-
CO, IN EAM COLONIAM MISSO VT REGIONIS SI-
TVM DILIGENTER OBSERVARET

NVNC AVTEM PRIMVM LATIO DONATA A
C. C. A.
CVM GRATIA ET PRIVILEGIO CAES. MA.TIS SPEC.LI
AD QVADRIENNIVM.

FRANCÓFORTI AD MOENVM
TYPIS IOANNIS WECHELI, SVMTIBVS VERO THEODORI
DE BRY ANNO CIƆ IƆ XC.
VENALES REPERIVNTVR IN OFFICINA SIGISMVNDI FEIRABENDII

of what White had drawn in pictures. It had none of the legendary "marvels" made up or imagined by so many early travelers. But there were wonders enough. Although Hariot's report was published in 1588, like White's drawings it was passed from hand to hand even before that.

It was from Hariot and White that the English gained the entrancing picture of Virginia that led to one more great effort to set up a permanent colony there.

Thomas Hariot published his "Briefe and True Report of the New Found Land of Virginia" in 1588. This is the title page of Theodore de Bry's 1590 reprint, for which the engravings from White's watercolors were made. It is these engravings that appear as illustrations of Indian life in this book. (RARE BOOK DIVISION, THE NEW YORK PUBLIC LIBRARY, ASTOR, LENOX AND TILDEN FOUNDATIONS)

Chapter IV

Raleigh began his new plans as soon as Drake returned with Lane and his colony. This time the colony would be truly self-governing, and would include men, women, and children. Each colonist would pay part of the cost and get a large grant of land. The colony would receive a charter as a corporation, THE GOVERNOR AND ASSISTANTS OF THE CITY OF RALEIGH IN VIRGINIA. John White, the artist, who had been in the 1584 exploration with Amadas and Barlowe as well as in Lane's colony, was made governor. He had twelve "assistants" who would serve as the governing body. One of them was his son-in-law, Ananias Dare. Another was Simon Fernandez, the Portuguese pilot who had so often been to America and who was now an English citizen.

It was agreed that they would settle in the Chesapeake Bay area, probably on the peninsula between the James and York rivers in what is now the city of Hampton, Virginia. But they would stop by Roanoke Island and leave new supplies for the fifteen men Grenville had left the year before. Or perhaps they might take those men aboard to join the Chesapeake settlement.

The expedition had trouble from the beginning. It did not leave England until May, 1587, late in the season. There was only one large ship, the *Lion*, a small flyboat, and a smaller pinnace. White was the chief of the expedition, but Fernandez was the chief pilot and sailing master, with authority over the voyage and the handling of the ships. The two men quarreled constantly. White was a better artist than a leader of men and was never able to assert his authority.

Although Fernandez had probably invested funds in the colony and was one of the "assistants," he never intended to settle there himself, as his interest was primarily financial, and more money was made from privateering than colonizing. War with Spain was now in the open after Drake's raids of the year before, and any Spanish ship was fair game.

As usual, they sailed first to the Caribbean. The *Lion* and the pinnace were separated from the flyboat on the voyage over. Fernandez insisted on staying in Caribbean waters for extra days, hunting in vain for Spanish treasure ships rather than taking on needed supplies.

It was July 7 before they finally sailed north for Roanoke and July 22 before they anchored at Port Ferdinando, the harbor named for Fernandez at what is now called Oregon Inlet. As soon as the *Lion* was secure, White and forty men left in the pinnace to find Grenville's men on Roanoke Island. As the pinnace was drawing away, Fernandez ordered the sailors to leave the settlers on Roanoke Island and not bring them back for the voyage to Chesapeake. He would have to leave soon to have any chance of catching the Spanish treasure fleet on the way home. And he was not willing, therefore, to go to Chesapeake. It was Roanoke or nothing.

65

White gave in. He could not force Fernandez and his sailors to obey him. Perhaps White himself felt more secure in the familiar Roanoke. Perhaps he was thinking of his daughter, whose baby was nearly due. In any event, he would have the pinnace and would be able to move to Chesapeake later if necessary.

After agreeing that the colony would stay, White continued to Roanoke in the pinnace to search for Grenville's men. When they landed they found the skeleton of a sailor lying across their path, tatters of his clothes still about the bones. It was nearly night, and they slept on the beach or in the pinnace. The next morning they walked to the north end of the island, where Lane's colony had had its forts and houses. They found what they had feared. The earth fort was torn down and the wooden palisade was burned. The houses were undamaged, but it was obvious that they had not been lived in for a long time. The vines of melons and pumpkins trailed through the doors and windows. A deer

A modern-day tableau of what the arriving colonists might have looked like as they landed at Roanoke. The scene is taken from a play, The Lost Colony, *which is produced by the Roanoke Island Historical Association with the cooperation of the state of North Carolina and the National Park Service. The play takes place on the shore where the original colonists landed.* (PHOTO BY AYCOCK BROWN)

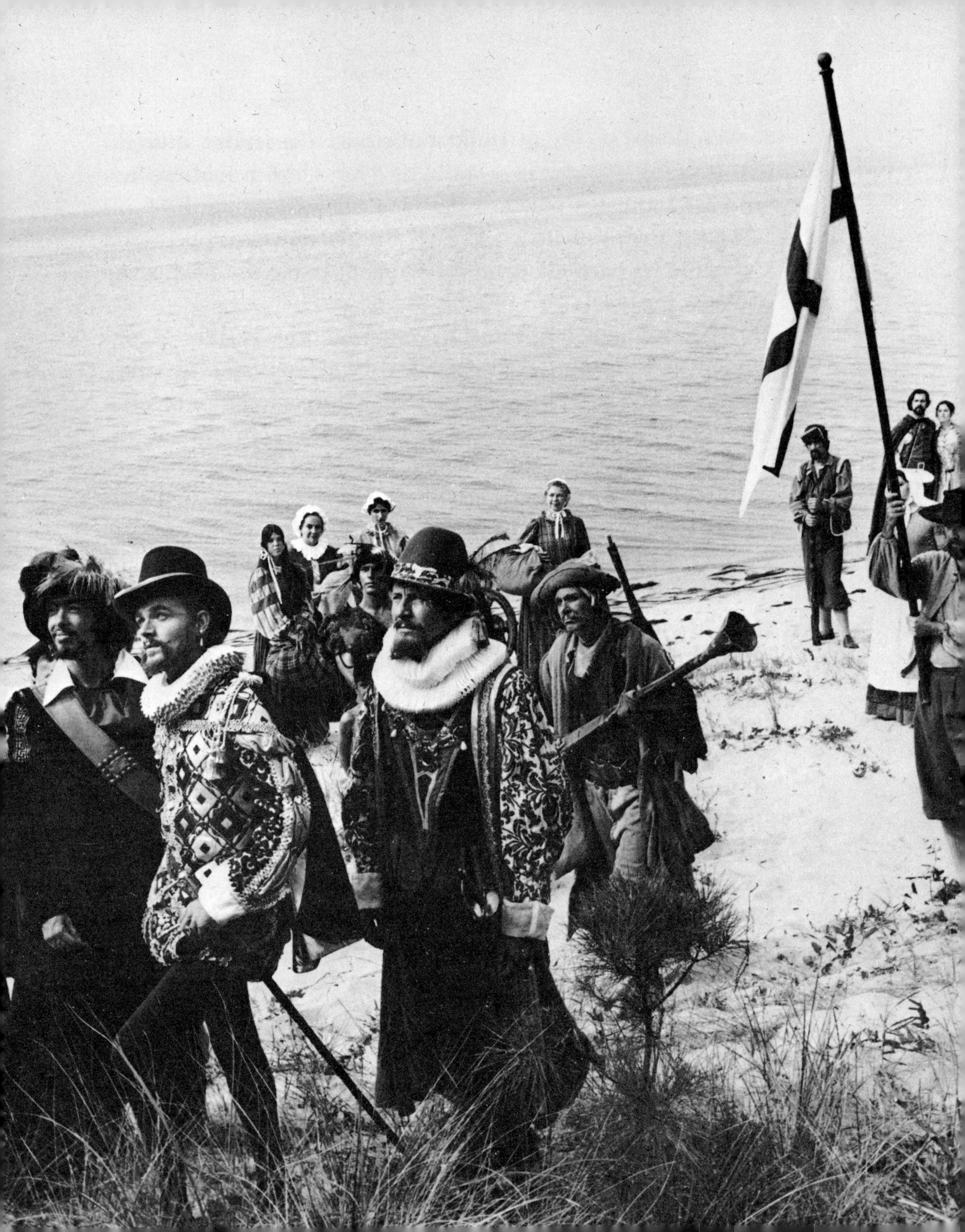

stood nibbling on the earth floor of a hut. The Indian village, too, was deserted. White realized that they would never again see Grenville's men.

He was thankful, however, that the houses were still there and could be repaired for the new colony. By the next day he had men busily at work on them.

The day following that they rejoiced. The smaller ship, the "flyboat," from which they had been separated for the entire voyage, reached Oregon Inlet. Now all the colonists were together.

Tragedy began to befall them almost immediately. On the twenty-eighth of July, three days after the flyboat arrived, White had had most of the colonists working busily repairing the huts. One of their leaders, George Howe, went off to hunt crabs a mile or two from the others. He stripped off his outer garments and went wading in the shallow waters on the sound side, probing for the crabs with a forked stick. As he went near a thicket of tall reeds growing along the marshy shore, an arrow whistled from the reeds and struck him. Before he could run, another dozen had pierced him. As he fell, Indians ran from their hiding place screaming war cries. They beat him to death with their clubs, and then ran to their canoes and paddled swiftly to the mainland before the colonists could catch them.

White realized that many of the Indians were now bitterly hostile to the white invaders of their island, and that he would have to restore friendship or else subdue them before he could have a peaceful settlement. Manteo had returned to the New World with the White colony, so White turned to him for help. White and other leaders went with Manteo to Croatoan, his home island. Even those Indians, who had always been friendly, at first grasped their bows to attack the English and then fearfully turned to run when they saw the English guns. Manteo called to them in their own language, and they turned. Seeing him they came back, timid but friendly. They were fearful above all that the English would take their food, for they had barely enough for themselves. White assured them that this time the English were well supplied and would not need food from the Indians, and that they only wanted to be friends again.

Manteo's people then welcomed them, but complained that Lane's men had more than once killed or wounded members of their tribe thinking them to be part of Wingina's hostile band. They asked for some sign by which the white men could be recognized as friendly.

Their meeting went on another day. The Croatoan Indians told them that those men of Wingina's tribe who had survived Lane's last attack still lived in the mainland village of Dasemonkepeuk. They were now led by Wanchese, the Indian who had gone to England with Manteo. On his return, Wanchese had joined Wingina and thrown his lot with his own people. It was they who had killed Howe and who, with some allies, had killed or driven off Grenville's men the year before. Manteo's people were able to describe exactly how Wanchese's men had driven away the Englishmen.

A de Bry engraving showing how the Indians cooked their fish. In his "Briefe and True Report," Hariot noted that unlike the Florida Indians, the Indians of North Carolina did not make any attempt to preserve their fish or game for winter storage. Until the arrival of the colonists, the food supply the year around was more than ample for the Indians' needs. (RARE BOOK DIVISION, THE NEW YORK PUBLIC LIBRARY, ASTOR, LENOX AND TILDEN FOUNDATIONS)

Thirty Indians had hidden themselves around the English village. Then two of them, pretending to be unarmed, had come into the open and invited two unarmed Englishmen to come and talk. When they did, the Indians had seized one of them, pulled concealed clubs from their cloaks, and killed him. The other Indians then leaped from their cover and fired a hail of arrows into the surprised Englishmen. The white men managed to run into the palisaded house within the earth fort. But the Indians threw burning brands or fired burning arrows into the fort and set the building aflame. The English had come running out, fighting their way through the Indians and the dense wood toward the water's edge. In this desperate skirmish one Indian and one Englishman were killed. Nine survivors had reached a boat and rowed down the beach to a nearby creek. Here they picked up the four remaining Englishmen and rowed to a small island just north of Oregon Inlet. They had left subsequently, and none of Manteo's people knew where they had gone or what had become of them.

White proposed to Manteo's people that they should go to the mainland Indians and assure them the white men would do them no harm and wanted only peace. Both sides should forgive and forget all past injuries and live as friends. Manteo's people agreed and promised to bring the leaders of the mainland tribes to Roanoke for a conference no later than August 6.

That day came and went, and then another. White took this to mean that the Indians refused to talk and were determined to fight. He decided to revenge the death of Howe and of Grenville's men, and once more to "teach the Indians a lesson." With twenty-five of his followers he rowed silently across the sound at midnight to the mainland near Dasemonkepeuk. They circled behind the village and fired into the Indians, driving them toward the water and hoping to destroy them. The startled natives ran into the reeds near the water, screaming that they were friends.

And so they were. Wanchese and his followers had abandoned the village and fled after killing Howe. Hearing this, Manteo's tribe had come to gather the melons and corn that had been left. It was Manteo's people who were there that night.

At least one of them was killed, which made Manteo angry with his English friends. But he was finally persuaded that it was a mistake that would not have happened if the leaders of his tribe had come to Roanake when they had promised and had explained that Wanchese's tribe had disappeared.

White then hoped to deal with the Indians through Manteo. Carrying out an idea of Raleigh's, they baptized Manteo as a Christian on August 13, and named him Lord of Roanoke and Dasemonkepeuk. They hoped that with English support they could make him chief of all the nearby Indians. Whether or not the plan succeeded we do not know. But it is not likely that the Indians truly recognized a leader named by the whites and carrying out the white men's wishes.

Time was passing, and Fernandez was ready to return.

The colonists were busy writing last letters home and collecting shells and other objects from the new land to send back to their friends. The sailors were cleaning and caulking the ships and loading fresh water and wood.

In one hut there was no time for such preparations. Eleanor Dare's time had come and on August 18 she bore a girl who was christened Virginia on the following Sunday. A few days later another baby was born — to Dyonis and Margery Harvey.

During these days the leaders of the colony were engaged in a long dispute. All were agreed that at least one leader should return with Fernandez to arrange for the earliest possible expedition to bring more food, supplies, and settlers. But no one wanted to be the one to go. Christopher Cooper at first agreed but then changed his mind. Finally all the other leaders insisted that White himself should make the trip. He did not want to go, because he thought he would be accused of cowardice, leading people to the New World and not being willing to stay himself. But finally he agreed to go if the colonists would sign a statement that he went unwillingly and only at their insistence.

This they did. White kissed his daughter and new granddaughter farewell, placed the possessions he was leaving in chests, and hurriedly packed for the return. On the morning of August 27 he was taken to Oregon Inlet in the pinnace and there boarded the flyboat. The next day they weighed anchor and sailed for England.

Chapter V

As the ships pulled away, the Roanoke colony passed into history. There were 116 of them left: 88 men, 17 women, 9 boys and girls, and the two new babies born in America. We know all their names, good English names: Bailey, Dare, Cooper, Stevens, Sampson, Harvey, Wills, Brook, White, Bright, Taylor, Sole, Cotsmuir, Pratt, Howe, Johnson, Warner, Cage, Jones, Tydway, Vickers, English, Tappan, Berry, Spendlove, Hemmington, Butler, Powell, Newton, Coleman, Graham, Bennett, Gibbs, Stilman, Wilkinson, Little, Willis, Martin, Patterson, Sutton, Farve, Bridger, Jones, Savage, Burden, Hynde, Ellis, Brown, Myllet, Smith, Kemme, Harris, Tavener, Ernest, Johnson, Starte, Darige, Lucas, Archard, Wright, Lacy, Cheven, Hewett, Baird, Glane, Pierce, Merrimoth, Dutton, Allen, Waters, Arthur, Chapman, Clement, Little, Wildey, Wotton, Bishop, Rufoote, Tomkins, Dorrell, Florrie, Milton, Payne, Harris, Lawrence, Warren, Mannering, Humphrey, Smart, Withers, Nichols, Phevens, Borden, Scott.

Their names are all we know of them now. No one came to look for them after White abandoned the search in 1590.

We can make some good guesses. They probably stayed at Roanoke for at least one year and perhaps two. Vines overgrew the huts used by Grenville's men in the time, less than a year, between their flight and the coming of the new colony. Yet in 1590 White does not record the site as overgrown. The CRO and CROATOAN were apparently still clear and not weathered or overgrown with vines or new bark. But his armor dug up by the Indians had nearly rusted through. Probably they stayed until their food was exhausted and they had given up hope for the promised relief expedition in 1588. Very likely they left in the winter of 1588-89.

They do not seem to have been killed or driven out at arrow point like Grenville's men. No cross was cut to show distress, and they had time to dismantle their houses and bury their chests with care. They probably took the planks from the houses so that they could rebuild them elsewhere. They obviously planned to return later for the buried chests.

No doubt after a year or more of waiting in vain for new supplies, they were faced with starvation — the old supplies were gone and they were not yet skilled enough in growing corn and beans and pumpkins or hunting and fishing to supply themselves. Hunger probably forced their move.

There is little reason to doubt that it was indeed to Croatoan they went. It was the nearest refuge where friendly Indians might give them food. They may well have been there when White came in 1590. The ships of that expedition had anchored well out to sea off Cape Hatteras before they came to Roanoke and had sent boats toward the inlet to take soundings. But if the colonists were at the village of

Croatoan on the sound side, they may have been totally unaware that their would-be rescuers were just a few miles off shore.

If they did indeed go to Croatoan, the mist of history closes over them there. They may have stayed and intermarried with the Indians. Over a century later the explorer John Lawson, writing in 1709, said he saw the ruins of the fort on Roanoke and found some guns and coins there. And he said the surviving Indians of the Hatteras area claimed to have white ancestors.

Or perhaps the colonists sailed in the pinnace in a desperate effort to reach England and were lost at sea. Or perhaps the Indians, driven themselves by hunger, killed the unwelcome guests or drove them elsewhere. From time to time discoveries have been reported of stones or markers carved with names or dates or messages that would tell us where the colonists went, but none have proved to be genuine. Time has drawn its veil over all the bold men and women of that heroic age. No one knows, or is ever likely to know, what actually happened to the colonists. Hawkins and Drake both died of fever in Caribbean ports in the same unlucky voyage, Hawkins in 1595, Drake in January, 1596. Elizabeth reigned for 45 years but was herself, in Raleigh's

An aerial view of the star-shaped Ralph Lane Fort as it has been restored today by the National Park Service of North Carolina. (COURTESY OF NATIONAL PARK SERVICE)

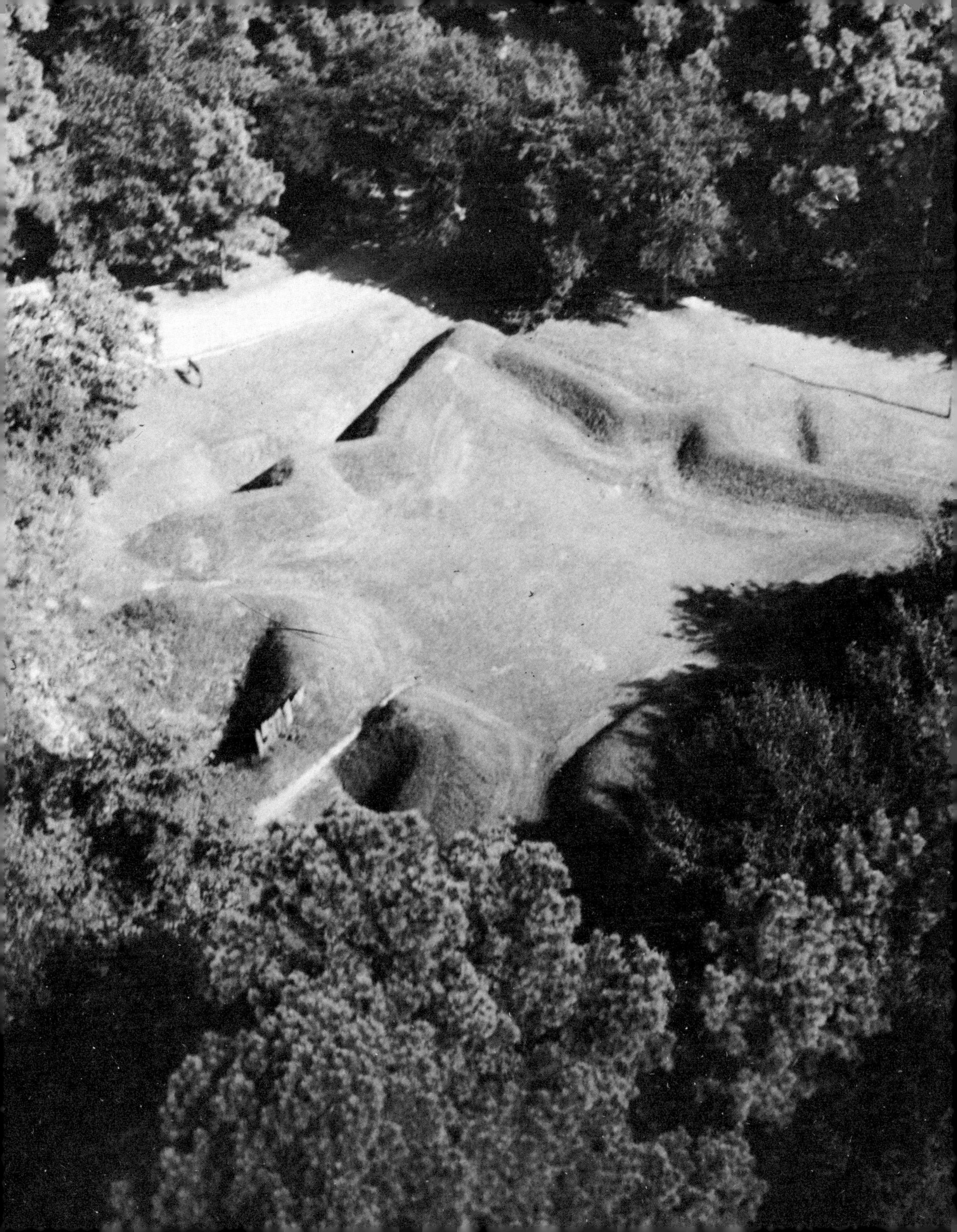

On this site, in July-August, 1585 (O.S.), colonists, sent out from England by Sir Walter Raleigh, built a fort, called by them

"THE NEW FORT IN VIRGINIA."

These colonists were the first settlers of the English race in America. They returned to England in July, 1586, with Sir Francis Drake.

Near this place was born, on the 18th of August, 1587,

VIRGINIA DARE,

the first child of English parents born in America — daughter of Ananias Dare and Eleanor White, his wife, members of another band of colonists, sent out by Sir Walter Raleigh in 1587.

On Sunday, August 20, 1587, Virginia Dare was baptized. Manteo, the friendly chief of the Hatteras Indians, had been baptized on the Sunday preceding. These baptisms are the first known celebrations of a Christian Sacrament in the territory of the thirteen original United States.

1896

words, "surprised by time" and died in 1603. Raleigh as an old man survived a last half-mad expedition to seek gold in the mountains of South America behind the jungles of the Orinoco. But he survived only to return to England and be beheaded in 1618 on an absurd charge of treason.

We know how the great men of that age came to their ends, but we do not know where in the Carolina wilderness the Roanoke settlers came to theirs. That fact, however, does not lessen their achievement. They were the first Englishmen to come to the New World with their wives and children, not to explore and return, but to live, they and their children and their children's children. They were the first people who came from England to be Americans.

After a delay because of the war with Spain, England returned in 1607 to colonize the New World. It was by then a matter for London merchants to plan and finance rather than for west country adventurers. But they used the same plan of organization Raleigh had formed. And they went to the Chesapeake, where he had intended the 1587 settlers to go. At Jamestown they finally achieved that permanent colony that so many had died to found at Roanoke. America had begun.

The site of Raleigh's colony on Roanoke is now a National

A plaque at Manteo, North Carolina, commemorating the landing of the colonists and the birth of Virginia Dare.
(COURTESY OF NATIONAL PARK SERVICE)

An aerial view of the waterside theater where The Lost Colony *is performed, and the Ralph Lane Fort at Fort Raleigh National Historic Site on Roanoke Island.* (PHOTO BY AYCOCK BROWN)

Historic Site, administered by the Park Service. The earth fort of 1585 has been excavated and restored. A nature path exhibits the plants and trees described by Hariot, and a museum shows typical weapons and costumes and equipment of the time, with prints of John White's paintings.

Nearby, at an outdoor theater on the water's edge, a pageant — "The Lost Colony" — has been presented on summer nights since the 350th anniversary of the colony in 1937. Night after night, under the stars, by the lapping of the waves in the sound, Elizabeth reigns again, and Raleigh plans, Manteo helps, and Wingina darkly broods. The Indians dance once more, the colonists sing English songs and hymns to build a memory of home around them in the wilderness. Eleanor Dare again brings her daughter, Virginia, to be baptized. And all on the very ground they trod. At the play's end, the actors march off into the veiling night, as the colonists they portray had done nearly four hundred years ago.

Index

Amadas, Philip:
  on 1584 expedition, 23, 25, 28, 35, 36, 45, 46
  on 1585 expedition, 39, 41-43
  mentioned, 38, 57, 64
Armada, Spanish, 4
Atlantic crossing routes, 35, 39

Barlowe, Arthur:
  on 1584 expedition, 23, 25, 28, 32-33, 35, 36, 45, 46
  mentioned, 38, 39, 57, 64
  quoted, 33
  visits Roanoke, 32-33
Brief and True Report of the New Found Land of Virginia (Hariot), 61
Bry, Theodore de, 61

Cadiz, Spain, Drake in, 15
Cape Fear, 25
Cape Hatteras, 25, 51, 75, 76
Caribbean:
  English piracy in, 15, 23, 55
  Spanish colonization of, 11, 54
Cartagena, Drake's looting of, 55
Central America, Spanish colonization of, 11, 54

Chesapeake Bay, 45-46, 59, 79
  exploration of, 48
  plans for colony at, 46, 55, 56, 64
  plans for colony abandoned by Fernandez, 65-66
Chowan River, 48-49, 55
Columbus, Christopher, 11
Cooper, Christopher, 73
Cornwall, England, 13
Croatoan (village), 4-5, 7, 69, 75-76
  Lane's men at, 51-52, 55

Dare, Ananias, 64
Dare, Eleanor, 3, 66, 73
Dare, Virginia, 3, 73
Dasemonkepeuk (village), 51, 69, 72
Drake, Sir Francis, 15, 57, 64, 65, 76
  at Roanoke, 55-56

Elizabeth I, Queen, 3, 11, 76
  and New World colonization, 20-22, 38, 39
  Raleigh and, 20, 39
Elizabeth, the, 39

83

England:
  under Elizabeth I, 11
  exploration of New World, 20, 23-36, 41, 48-51
  New World colonization by, 22, 38, 43-45, 57, 64, 79
  ships of, 13-15, 23
  war with Spain, 4, 65, 79
English piracy, 15, 23, 35-36, 55, 57, 65
Expeditions, English, 15, 20, 76, 79
  Amadas and Barlowe (1584), 23-36
  Drake's, to Caribbean, 55-56
  under Grenville (1585), 39-46
  under Grenville (1586), 56-59
  White's (1587), 64-73
  White's (1590), 3-10, 74, 75

Fernandez, Simon, 25, 28, 39
  on 1587 expedition, 64, 65, 66, 72
Francis, the, 56

Galleons, Spanish, 13-15
Gilbert, Sir Humphrey, 18-22
Granganimeo, 29-32, 43
Grenville, Sir Richard, 39
  first expedition to Roanoke (1585), 39, 41, 43, 45, 46
  return to Roanoke (1586), 56-57, 59
  mentioned, 54, 55, 65, 66, 68, 69, 72, 74, 75

Hakluyt, Richard, 38
Hariot, Thomas, 38, 39, 43, 59, 61-63, 81
  his report on New World, 61
Harvey, Dyonis, 73
Harvey, Margery, 73
Havana, 55
Hawkins, Sir John, 15, 76
Hopewell, the, 7
Howe, George, 68, 69, 71, 72

Indians, of Roanoke area, 28-33, 43-45
  English relations with, 32-33, 41-43, 48, 57-59, 68-72
  hostilities with, 49-54, 68, 71, 72
  trips to England by, 36, 39, 56, 68
Isthmus of Panama, 55, 56

Jamestown, 57, 79

Lane, Ralph, 64, 66
  in charge of Roanoke colony, 45, 46, 48-59
  explorations by, 48-51
  harsh Indian policy of, 48, 49, 52-54, 57, 69
Lawson, John, 76
Lion, the, 64, 65
Lynnhaven Bay, 48

Mann's Harbor, 51

Manteo, Chief, 5, 43, 52, 68-72
  baptism of, 72
  first trip to England, 36, 39
  second trip to England, 56, 68
Menatonon, Chief, 49
Mexico, Spanish colonization of, 11, 54
Moonlight, the, 7

National Historic Site at Roanoke, 79-81
Newfoundland, 20, 22, 23

Oregon Inlet, 25, 46, 51, 55, 56, 65
Outer Banks islands, 25, 32, 35

Panama, Isthmus of, 55, 56
Peru, Spanish colonization of, 11, 54
Piracy, English, 15, 23, 35-36, 55, 57, 65
Port Ferdinando, 65
Puerto Rico, 1585 expedition stopover in, 39

Raleigh, Sir Walter, 15, 18-22, 28, 45, 72, 76
  background of, 18
  death of, 79
  description of, 15
  Elizabeth I and, 20, 39
  expedition to South America, 79
  and New World colonization, 20, 22-23, 35, 36-38, 39, 55, 56, 64, 79
Roanoke Island, 35, 57
  description of, 32-33
  English settlement on, 43-46, 48, 51-52, 57, 64, 65-73, 74, 79
  first English visit to (1584), 32-33
  names of colonists, 74
  National Historic Site, 79-81
  speculations on fate of colonists, 74-76
  unsuited for privateer base, 45, 54-55
  White's return to (1590), 3-10, 74
Roanoke River, exploratory expedition, 48-51

St. Augustine, Fla., Drake's seizure of, 55, 56
Santo Domingo, Drake's looting of, 55
Sea dogs, 15. *See also* Piracy
Shakespeare, William, 11
Shipping:
  English, 13-15, 23
  Spanish galleons, 13-15
Shipping routes, across Atlantic, 35, 39
South America:
  Raleigh's expedition to, 79

85

Spanish colonization of, 11, 54
Spain:
   colonization in New World, 11, 54
   English piracy against, 15, 23, 35-36, 55, 57, 65
   ships of, 13-15
   war with England, 4, 65, 79
Spanish Armada, 4

Tiger, the, 39, 41
Trinidad, 7, 10

Virginia, 63, 64
   Hariot's report on, 61

Wanchese, Chief, 36, 39, 43, 69, 72
White, John:
   drawings of, 59-61, 63, 81
   on 1584 expedition, 23
   on 1585 expedition, 39
   leads 1587 expedition, 64-73
   relations with Indians, 68-72
   return to Roanoke (1590), 3-10, 74
Wingina, King, 29, 59, 69
   allows English settlement, 43-45, 46
   becomes hostile toward English settlers, 48-49, 51, 52
   death of, 54
Wococon Inlet, 41

About the Author

Dan Lacy was born in Newport News, Virginia, but grew up in Rocky Mount, which is a town in northeastern Carolina not far from Roanoke Island and the site of the Lost Colony. After graduating from the University of North Carolina with an M.A. degree in southern history, he taught at the university for several years. He later was with the National Archives as Assistant Archivist of the United States and also served as the Deputy Chief Assistant Librarian of the Library of Congress.

From 1953 though 1966, Mr. Lacy was the managing director of the American Book Publishers Council. He is now a senior vice-president of a major New York publishing company.

His other books include THE MEANING OF THE AMERICAN REVOLUTION and THE WHITE USE OF BLACKS IN AMERICA.

Lawsonville School Library
E. S. E. A. Title IV
1976-77